W9-BMZ-509

Study Guide for Praxis *Social Studies* Constructed-Response Tests

▶ ▶ ▶ ▶ ▶ ▶ ▶ ▶ ▶ ▶ ▶ ▶

A PUBLICATION OF EDUCATIONAL TESTING SERVICE

Table of Contents
Study Guide for Praxis *Social Studies* Constructed-Response Tests

▶ ▶ ▶ ▶ ▶ ▶ ▶ ▶ ▶ ▶ ▶ ▶

Section 1

Chapter 1

Introduction to the Praxis *Social Studies* Constructed-Response Tests
and Suggestions for Using This Study Guide 1

Chapter 2

Background Information on The Praxis Series™ Assessments 7

Chapter 3

Succeeding on the *Social Studies* Constructed-Response Tests 11

Section 2

Chapter 4

Preparing for the *Social Studies: Analytical Essays* Test 21

Chapter 5

Practice Test—S*ocial Studies: Analytical Essays* 33

Chapter 6

Sample Responses and How They Were Scored—*Social Studies:
Analytical Essays* 51

Section 3

Chapter 7

Preparing for the *Social Studies: Interpretation of Materials* Test 69

Chapter 8

Practice Test—*Social Studies: Interpretation of Materials* 79

Chapter 9

Sample Responses and How They Were Scored—*Social Studies:
Interpretation of Materials* 99

Section 4

Section 5

Chapter 1
Introduction to the *Social Studies* Constructed-Response Tests and Suggestions for Using This Study Guide

▶ ▶ ▶ ▶ ▶ ▶ ▶ ▶ ▶ ▶ ▶ ▶

Introduction to the *Social Studies* Constructed-Response Tests

The *Social Studies* constructed-response tests are designed for prospective secondary social studies teachers. The tests are designed to reflect current standards for knowledge, skills, and abilities in teaching social studies. ETS works in collaboration with teacher educators, higher education content specialists, and accomplished practicing teachers in the field of social studies to keep the tests updated and representative of current standards.

This study guide covers four different tests of social studies. Because the tests are *constructed-response* tests, you are asked to answer questions or groups of questions by writing out your responses. Your responses will *not* be graded on the basis of how they succeed as essays. Instead, your responses will be graded on the basis of how well they demonstrate an understanding of social studies.

This study guide covers the following tests:

Test Name and Code	Length of Test	Number and Format of Questions
Social Studies: Analytical Essays (0082)	60 minutes	Two essay questions: I. United States: History or Contemporary Issues II. World: History or Contemporary Issues
Social Studies: Interpretation of Materials (0083)	60 minutes	Five two-part essay questions; each essay question involves identification/comprehension and interpretation/application in a short-essay format: I. United States History II. World History III. Government/Civics IV. Geography V. Economics

Test Name and Code	Length of Test	Number and Format of Questions
Social Studies: Pedagogy (0084)	60 minutes	Two five-part essay questions, based on a case-study format: Case Study I—Two-Week History Unit • Subject Matter Topics • Social Studies Concepts • Metaphor/Analogy/Historical Parallel • Questions for Class Discussion Case Study II—Single-Period Social Science Unit • Lesson • Objective • Teaching Strategy • Evaluation
Social Studies: Interpretation and Analysis (0085)	120 minutes	Five short-answer questions based on materials such as maps, charts, and excerpts, and two essay questions addressing fundamental concepts and interdisciplinary relationships: I. History: United States and World II. Social Science: Government III. Geography, and Economics IV. Social Studies Analysis: United States V. Social Studies Analysis: World

How to Use This Study Guide

This study guide gives you instruction, practice, and test-taking tips to help you prepare for taking the *Social Studies* constructed-response tests. In chapter 2 you will find a discussion of The Praxis Series™—what it is and how the tests in The Praxis Series are developed. In chapter 3 you will find information on how to succeed on constructed-response tests. Then chapters 4, 5, and 6 (for the *Social Studies: Analytical Essays* test), 7, 8, and 9 (for the *Social Studies: Interpretation of Materials* test), 10, 11, and 12 (for the *Social Studies: Pedagogy* test), and 13, 7, 4, 8, 5, 9, and 6 (for the *Social Studies: Interpretation and Analysis* test) will help you prepare for the test, give you the chance to take a practice test, and show you sample responses and how they were scored.

So where should you start? Well, all users of this book will probably want to begin with the following two steps:

- **Become familiar with the test content.** Note what the appropriate chapter of the book (4, 7, or 10) says about the topics covered in the test you plan to take.

- **Consider how well you know the content in each subject area.** Perhaps you already know that you need to build up your skills in a particular area. If you're not sure, skim over the chapter that covers test content (4, 7, or 10) to see what topics the test covers. If you encounter material that feels unfamiliar or difficult, fold down page corners or insert sticky notes to remind yourself to spend extra time in these sections.

Also, all users of this book will probably want to end with these two steps:

- **Familiarize yourself with test taking.** Chapter 3 explains how constructed-response tests are scored and contains valuable tips on how to succeed on a test in this format. When you feel you understand the format, you can simulate the experience of the test by taking a practice test (chapter 5, 8, or 11) within the specified time limits. Choose a time and place where you will not be interrupted or distracted. After you complete the test, look at the appropriate chapter (6, 9, or 12) to see sample responses that scored well, scored poorly, or scored in-between. By examining these sample responses, you can focus on the aspects of your own practice response that were successful and unsuccessful. This knowledge will help you plan any additional studying you might need.

- **Register for the test and consider last-minute tips.** Consult www.ets.org/praxis/index.html to learn how to register for the test, and review the checklist in chapter 14 to make sure you are ready for the test.

What you do between these first steps and these last steps depends on whether you intend to use this book to prepare on your own or as part of a class or study group.

Using this book to prepare on your own

If you are working by yourself to prepare for a *Social Studies* constructed-response test, you may find it helpful to fill out the Study Plan Sheet in appendix A. This work sheet will help you to focus on what topics you need to study most, identify materials that will help you study, and set a schedule for doing the studying. The last item is particularly important if you know you tend to put off work.

Using this book as part of a study group

People who have a lot of studying to do sometimes find it helpful to form a study group with others who are preparing toward the same goal. Study groups give members opportunities to ask questions and get detailed answers. In a group, some members usually have a better understanding of certain topics, while others in the group may be better at other topics. As members take turns explaining concepts to each other, everyone builds self-confidence. If the group encounters a question that none of the members can answer well, the members can go as a group to a teacher or other expert and get answers efficiently. Because study groups schedule regular meetings, group members study in a more disciplined fashion. They also gain emotional support. The group should be large enough so that various people can contribute various kinds of knowledge, but small enough so that it stays focused. Often, three to six people is a good size.

Here are some ways to use this book as part of a study group:

- **Plan the group's study program.** Parts of the Study Plan Sheet in appendix A can help to structure your group's study program. By filling out the first five columns and sharing the work sheets, everyone will learn more about your group's mix of abilities and about the resources (such as textbooks) that members can share with the group. In the sixth column ("Dates planned for study of content"), you can create an overall schedule for your group's study program.

- **Plan individual group sessions.** At the end of each session, the group should decide what specific topics will be covered at the next meeting and who will present each topic. Use the topics in the chapter that covers the test you will take.

- **Prepare your presentation for the group.** When it's your turn to be presenter, prepare something that's more than a lecture. Write two or three original questions to pose to the group. Practicing writing actual questions can help you better understand the topics covered on the test as well as the types of questions you will encounter on the test. It will also give other members of the group extra practice at answering questions.

- **Take the practice test together.** The idea of the practice test is to simulate an actual administration of the test, so scheduling a test session with the group will add to the realism and will also help boost everyone's confidence.

- **Learn from the results of the practice test.** For each test, score each other's answer sheets. Read the chapter that contains the corresponding sample responses and shows how they were scored (6, 9, or 12), and then try to follow the same guidelines that the test scorers use.

  - *Be as critical as you can.* You're not doing your study partner a favor by letting him or her get away with an answer that does not cover all parts of the question adequately.

  - *Be specific.* Write *comments* that are as detailed as the comments made in chapter 6, 9, or 12 by the scoring leader. Indicate *where and how* your study partner is doing a poor job of answering the question. Writing notes in the margins of the answer sheet may also help.

  - *Also be supportive.* Include comments that point out what your study partner got right and that therefore earned points.

  Then plan one or more study sessions based on aspects of the questions on which group members performed poorly. For example, each group member might be responsible for rewriting one paragraph of a response in which someone else did an inadequate job of answering the question.

Whether you decide to study alone or with a group, remember that the best way to prepare is to have an organized plan. The plan should set goals based on specific topics and skills that you need to learn, and it should commit you to a realistic set of deadlines for meeting these goals. Then you need to discipline yourself to stick with your plan and accomplish your goals on schedule.

Chapter 2

Background Information on The Praxis Series™ Assessments

▶ ▶ ▶ ▶ ▶ ▶ ▶ ▶ ▶ ▶ ▶ ▶

What Are The Praxis Series™ Subject Assessments?

The Praxis Series Subject Assessments are designed by ETS to assess your knowledge of the area of education in which you plan to work, and they are a part of the licensing procedure in many states. This study guide covers assessments that test your knowledge of the actual content related to your intended specialization. Your state has adopted The Praxis Series tests because it wants to be certain that you have achieved a specified level of mastery of your subject area before it grants you a license to work in a school.

The Praxis Series tests are part of a national testing program, meaning that the tests covered in this study guide are used in more than one state. The advantage of taking Praxis tests is that if you want to practice in another state that uses The Praxis Series tests, that state will recognize your scores. Passing scores are set by states, however, so if you are planning to apply for licensure in another state, you may find that passing scores are different. You can find passing scores for all states that use The Praxis Series tests either on-line at www.ets.org/praxis/prxstate.html or in the *Understanding Your Praxis Scores* pamphlet, available either in your college's School of Education or by calling (609) 771-7395. You can also find it at www.ets.org/praxis/prxstate.html.

What Is Licensure?

Licensure in any area—medicine, law, architecture, accounting, cosmetology—is an assurance to the public that the person holding the license has demonstrated a certain level of competence. The phrase used in licensure is that the person holding the license *will do no harm*. In the case of licensing for educators, a license tells the public that the person holding the license can be trusted to educate children competently and professionally.

Because a license makes such a serious claim about its holder, licensure tests are usually quite demanding. In some fields licensure tests have more than one part and last for more than one day. Candidates for licensure in all fields plan intensive study as part of their professional preparation: some join study groups, while others study alone. But preparing to take a licensure test is, in all cases, a professional activity. Because it assesses your entire body of knowledge or skill for the field you want to enter, preparing for a licensure exam takes planning, discipline, and sustained effort. Studying thoroughly is highly recommended.

Why Does My State Require The Praxis Series Subject Assessments?

Your state chose The Praxis Series Subject Assessments because the tests assess the breadth and depth of content—called the "domain" of the test—that your state wants its education professionals to have before they begin to work. The level of content knowledge, reflected in the passing score, is based on recommendations of panels of professionals and postsecondary educators in each subject area in each state. The state licensing agency and, in some states, the state legislature ratify the passing scores that have been recommended by panels of professionals. (See "What Are the Praxis Series Subject Assessments?" above for where to find your state's passing score.). Not all states use the same test modules, and even when they do, the passing scores can differ from state to state.

What Kinds of Tests Are The Praxis Series Subject Assessments?

Two kinds of tests comprise The Praxis Series Subject Assessments: multiple-choice (for which you select your answer from a list of choices) and constructed-response (for which you write a response of your own). Multiple-choice tests can survey a wider domain because they can ask more questions in a limited period of time. Constructed-response tests have far fewer questions, but the questions require you to demonstrate the depth of your knowledge in the area covered.

What Do the Tests measure?

The Praxis Series Subject Assessments are tests of content knowledge. They measure your understanding of the subject area that will be your specialization. The multiple-choice tests measure a broad range of knowledge across your content area. The constructed-response tests measure your ability to explain in depth a few essential topics in your subject area. The content-specific pedagogy tests, most of which are constructed-response, measure your understanding of how to teach certain fundamental concepts in your field. The tests do not measure actual teaching ability, however. They measure your knowledge of your subject and (for classroom specializations) of how to teach it. The professionals in your field who help us design and write these tests, and the states that require these tests, do so in the belief that knowledge of subject area is the first requirement for licensing. Your ability to perform in an actual school is a skill that is measured in other ways: Observation, videotaped teaching, or portfolios typically are used by states to measure this ability. Education combines many complex skills, only some of which can be measured by a single test. The Praxis Series Subject Assessments are designed to measure how thoroughly you understand the material in the subject areas for which you want to be licensed.

How Were These Tests Developed?

ETS began the development of The Praxis Series Subject Assessments with a survey. For each subject, professionals around the country in various educational situations were asked to judge which knowledge and skills a beginning practitioner in that subject needs to possess. Professors in schools of education who prepare professionals were asked the same questions. These responses were ranked in order of importance and sent out to hundreds of professionals for review. All of the responses to these surveys (called "job analysis surveys") were analyzed to summarize the judgments of these professionals. From their consensus, we developed the specifications for the multiple-choice and constructed-response tests. Each subject area had a committee of practitioners and postsecondary educators who wrote these specifications (guidelines). The specifications were reviewed and eventually approved by professionals. From the test specifications, groups of practitioners and professional test developers created test questions.

When your state adopted The Praxis Series Subject Assessments, local panels of practicing professionals and postsecondary educators in each subject area met to examine the tests question by question and evaluate each question for its relevance to beginning professionals in your state. This is called a "validity study." A test is considered "valid" for a job if it measures what people must know and be able to do on that job. For the test to be adopted in your state, professionals in your state must judge that it is valid.

These professionals also performed a "standard-setting study"; that is, they went through the tests question by question and decided, through a rigorous process, how many questions a beginning professional should be able to answer correctly. From this study emerged a recommended passing score. The final passing score was approved by your state's Department of Education.

In other words, throughout the development process, practitioners in the field of education—professionals and postsecondary educators—have determined what the tests would contain. The practitioners in your state determined which tests would be used for licensure in your subject area and helped decide what score would be needed to achieve licensure. This is how professional licensure works in most fields: those who are already licensed oversee the licensing of new practitioners. When you pass The Praxis Series Subject Assessments, you and the practitioners in your state can be assured that you have the knowledge required to begin practicing your profession.

Chapter 3
Succeeding on the *Social Studies* Constructed-Response Tests

▶ ▶ ▶ ▶ ▶ ▶ ▶ ▶ ▶ ▶ ▶ ▶

The goal of this chapter is to provide you with background information and general advice from experts so that you can improve your skills in writing answers to constructed-response questions, and specifically, the kinds of questions that appear on the *Social Studies* constructed-response tests. You will see advice from experts, the guidelines that are used when the test questions are scored, and background information on the scoring process.

Advice from the Experts

Scorers who have scored hundreds of real tests were asked to give advice to students taking the *Social Studies* constructed-response tests. The practical pieces of advice given below summarize the scorers' advice:

1. **Read through the question carefully before you answer it, and try to answer all parts of the question.**

   This seems simple, but many test takers fail to understand the question and to provide a complete response. If the question asks you to do three distinct things, don't respond to just one or two of those things. If the question asks for problems and solutions, don't describe just problems. No matter how well you write about one part of the question, the scorers cannot award you full credit unless you answer the question completely and correctly.

2. **Be direct and explicit in your response.**

   Your response must indicate to the scorers that you have a clear understanding of the relevant social studies issues. The scorers will not read into your response; they respond only to what you actually tell them. If something is not written or is implied only vaguely, they do not know that you know it and will not give you credit for it.

3. **Give a full and thorough response.**

   If the question asks you to "describe" or "discuss" something, keep that task in mind when composing your response; do not simply mention the concept by name or give a list. A discussion is superior to a brief identification.

4. **Keep your essay thematically focused.**

   Focus on analyzing the questions you are asked. Superior essays organize their information around answering the questions directly. Weaker essays tend to ramble around the topic. Your response should be driven by its arguments. State your themes clearly and keep them at the center of your discussion.

5. **Give a detailed response.**

   If you have specific, relevant knowledge—of events, names, time periods, places—do not be shy about sharing it. An essay rich in detail appears much more informed and impressive than one that is correct but trades in generalities.

6. Do not give incorrect information.

Do not write down as fact something you don't know to be true. Essays are graded holistically, and an otherwise decent, knowledgeable essay can be ruined by a large, fatal error or an accumulation of smaller ones. If you are in doubt, don't guess.

The Guidelines Used for Scoring the Test Questions

The General Scoring Guide for the *Social Studies: Analytical Essays* (0082) Test

The following guide provides the framework for scoring the constructed-response questions on the *Analytical Essays* test on a scale of 0 to 5.

Score		Comment
5	▪	Provides a full, insightful analysis, with logical, well-supported explanations and conclusions
	▪	Interprets the stimulus (if applicable) accurately and applies it effectively
	▪	Demonstrates a superior understanding of the subject, including interdisciplinary connections
	▪	Provides well-chosen and accurate factual information
	▪	Is well organized and very clear throughout
4	▪	Provides a substantial analysis, with logically developed explanations and conclusions
	▪	Interprets the stimulus (if applicable) accurately and applies it appropriately
	▪	Demonstrates a strong understanding of the subject
	▪	Provides relevant and accurate factual information, with very few significant errors
	▪	Is organized and clear
3	▪	Provides an analysis with generally logical explanations and conclusions
	▪	Interprets and applies the stimulus (if applicable) in a mostly accurate and appropriate way
	▪	Demonstrates an adequate understanding of the subject
	▪	Provides mostly relevant and accurate factual information (may have a few significant errors)
	▪	Is, for the most part, organized and clear

2
- Provides a limited analysis, with poorly developed explanations and conclusions
- Interprets and applies the stimulus (if applicable) with a lack of accuracy and appropriateness
- Demonstrates a limited understanding of the subject
- Lacks relevant and accurate factual information (may have significant errors)
- May be poorly organized or lack clarity

1
- Provides scarcely any analysis, logical explanations, or conclusions
- Misinterprets the stimulus (if applicable) and applies it inappropriately
- Demonstrates very little understanding of the subject
- Provides scarcely any relevant or accurate information (may have many significant errors)
- May be disorganized or confusing

0
- Completely inaccurate or inappropriate, blank, off topic, or only a restatement of the prompt

The General Scoring Guide for the *Social Studies: Interpretation of Materials* (0083) Test

The following guide provides the framework for scoring the constructed-response questions on the *Social Studies: Interpretation of Materials* test.

Each of the two questions has two parts and is given two scores, on a scale of 0 to 3.

Part 1 of the Question

<u>Score</u>	<u>Comment</u>

3 Accurate and complete:
- Shows a clear understanding of the stimulus
- Provides an accurate and complete response

2 Mostly accurate and complete:
- Shows an adequate understanding of the stimulus
- Provides a generally accurate and complete response

1 Inaccurate and incomplete:
- Shows little understanding of the stimulus
- Provides a basically inaccurate and incomplete response

0 Completely inaccurate or inappropriate, blank, off topic, or only a restatement of the prompt

Part 2 of the Question

Score	Comment

3 Accurate and complete:

- Provides the analysis required by the question
- Applies appropriate subject matter knowledge

2 Mostly accurate and complete:

- Provides most of the analysis required by the question
- Applies mostly appropriate subject matter knowledge

1 Inaccurate and incomplete:

- Provides little of the analysis required by the question
- Applies mostly inappropriate subject matter knowledge

0 Completely inaccurate or inappropriate, blank, off topic, or only a restatement of the prompt

The General Scoring Guide for the *Social Studies: Pedagogy* (0084) Test

Each response to a case study on the test consists of five parts. Test scorers rate each part of a response individually on a scale of 0 to 3. Therefore, the total number of points that a response can receive from a scorer is 15.

The following guide provides the framework for scoring the responses to case studies.

Score	Comment

3 Accurate and complete:

- Demonstrates a clear understanding of relevant subject matter and pedagogy
- Provides appropriate, accurate, and complete explanations and/or supporting information

2 Mostly accurate and complete:

- Demonstrates an adequate understanding of relevant subject matter and pedagogy
- Provides mostly appropriate, accurate, and complete explanations and/or supporting information

1 Inaccurate and incomplete:

- Demonstrates a weak understanding of subject matter and pedagogy
- Provides inappropriate and/or little support (when needed)

0 Completely inaccurate or inappropriate, blank, off topic, or only a restatement of the prompt

The General Scoring Guide for the *Social Studies: Interpretation and Analysis* (0085) Test

Each of the five short-answer questions in Part I has two parts and is given two scores, on a scale of 0 to 3. Each of the two essay questions in Part II is scored on the same scale of 0 to 3. In assigning these scores, the scorers use the following guide.

<u>Score</u>	<u>Comment</u>

3   Accurate and complete:

- Shows a thorough understanding of the stimulus
- Provides an accurate and complete response
- Provides the analysis required by the question
- Applies appropriate subject matter knowledge
- May contain minor errors

2   Mostly accurate and complete:

- Shows an adequate understanding of the stimulus
- Provides a mostly accurate and complete response
- Provides most of the analysis required by the question
- Applies mostly appropriate subject matter knowledge
- May contain significant errors

1   Inaccurate and incomplete

- Shows little understanding of the stimulus
- Provides a basically inaccurate and incomplete response
- Provides little of the analysis required by the question
- Applies mostly inappropriate subject matter knowledge
- May contain minor errors

0   Completely inaccurate or inappropriate, blank, off topic, or only a restatement of the prompt

Question-Specific Scoring Guides

After a question is developed, three or four knowledgeable experts develop ideas for "model answers." These model answers are used to develop a "Question-Specific Scoring Guide," which creates a list of specific examples that would receive various scores. This list contains examples of various answers, not all possible answers. These question-specific scoring guides, which are based on model answers, provide the basis for choosing the papers that serve as the benchmarks and sample papers used for training the scorers at the scoring session. During the scoring sessions, specific examples can be added to the scoring guide and papers can be added as samples for future readings.

Given the information above about how constructed responses are scored and what the scorers are looking for in successful responses, you are now ready to look at specific questions, suggestions of how to approach the questions, sample responses, and the scores given to those responses.

The Scoring Process

As you build your skills in writing answers to constructed-response questions, it is important to keep in mind the process used to score the tests. If you understand the process by which experts award scores, you will have a better context in which to think about your strategies for success.

The scoring session

After each test administration, test books are returned to ETS. The test booklets in which constructed-response answers are written are sent to the location of the scoring session.

The scoring sessions usually take place over two days. The sessions are led by "scoring leaders," highly qualified social studies teachers who have many years of experience scoring test questions. All of the remaining scorers are experienced social studies teachers and social studies teacher-educators. An effort is made to balance experienced scorers with newer scorers at each session; the experienced scorers provide continuity with past sessions, and the new scorers ensure that new ideas and perspectives are considered and that the pool of scorers remains large enough to cover the test's needs throughout the year.

At a typical scoring session, eight to twelve scorers are seated at three or four tables, with any new scorers distributed equally across all tables. One of the scoring leaders, the chief scorer or a table leader, sits at each table. The "chief scorer" is the person who has overall authority over the scoring session and who plays a variety of key roles in training and in ensuring consistent and fair scores. Table leaders assist the chief scorer with these responsibilities.

Preparing to train the scorers

Training scorers is a rigorous process, and it is designed to ensure that each response gets a score that is consistent both with the scores given to other papers and with the overall scoring philosophy and criteria established for the test when it was first designed.

The chief scorer first takes the scorers through a review of the "General Scoring Guide," which contains the overall criteria, stated in general terms, for awarding a score. The chief scorer also reviews and discusses—and, when there are new test questions, makes additions to—the question-specific scoring guides, which apply the rubrics in the general guide to each specific question on the test. The question-specific guides are not intended to cover every possible response the scorers will see. Rather, they are designed to give enough examples to guide the scorers in making accurate judgments about the variety of answers they will encounter.

To begin identifying appropriate training materials for an individual question, the chief scorer first reads through many responses from the bundles of responses to get a sense of the range of the responses. The chief scorer then chooses a set of "benchmarks," typically selecting two responses at each score level for each question. These benchmarks serve as representative of the kind of response that meets the criteria of each score level and are the foundation for score standards throughout the session.

The chief scorer then chooses a set of test-taker responses to serve as sample papers. These sample papers represent the wide variety of possible responses that the scorers might see. The sample papers will serve as the basis for practice scoring at the scoring session so that the scorers can rehearse how they will apply the scoring criteria before they begin.

The process of choosing a set of benchmark responses and a set of sample responses is followed systematically for each new question to be scored at the session. After the chief scorer is done with selections and discussions, the sets that have been chosen are photocopied and inserted into the scorers' folders for use in future sessions.

Training the scorers

For each question, the training session proceeds in the same way:

1. All scorers review the "General Scoring Guide" and the "Question-Specific Scoring Guide."

2. All scorers carefully read through the question.

3. The leaders guide the scorers through the set of benchmark responses, explaining in detail why each response received the score it did. Scorers are encouraged to ask questions and share their perspectives. All of the scorers are trained together to ensure uniformity in the application of the scoring criteria.

4. Scorers then practice on the set of sample responses chosen by the leaders. The leaders poll the scorers on what scores they would award and then lead a discussion to ensure that there is consensus about the scoring criteria and how they are to be applied.

5. When the leaders are confident that the scorers will apply the criteria consistently and accurately, the actual scoring begins.

Quality-control processes

There are a number of procedures that are designed to ensure that the accuracy of scoring is maintained during the scoring session and to ensure that each response receives as many points as the scoring criteria allow. The test books, for example, are designed so that any personal or specific information about the test taker, such as name and test center location, are never seen by the scorers. Additionally, each response is scored twice, with the first scorer's decision hidden from the second scorer. If the two scores for a paper are the same or differ by only one point, the scoring for that paper is considered complete and the test taker is awarded the sum of the two scores. If the two scores differ by more than one point, the response is scored by the chief scorer and the score is revised accordingly.

Another way of maintaining scoring accuracy is through "back-reading." Throughout the session, the chief scorer checks a random sample of scores awarded by scorers. If the chief scorer finds that a scorer is not applying the scoring criteria appropriately, that scorer is given more training and his or her scores are checked. The chief scorer also back-reads all responses that received scores differing by more than one point to ensure that every appropriate point has been awarded.

Finally, the scoring session is designed so that a number of different scorers contribute to any single test taker's score. This minimizes the effects of a scorer who might score slightly more rigorously or generously than other scorers.

The entire scoring process—standardized benchmarks and samples, general and specific scoring guides, adjudication procedures, back-reading, scorer statistics, and rotation of exams to a variety of scorers—is applied consistently and systematically at every scoring session to ensure comparable scores for each administration and across all administrations of the test.

Chapter 4
Preparing for the *Social Studies: Analytical Essays* Test

▶ ▶ ▶ ▶ ▶ ▶ ▶ ▶ ▶ ▶ ▶ ▶

The goal of this chapter is to provide you with strategies for reading, analyzing, and understanding the questions on the *Social Studies: Analytical Essays* test and then for outlining and writing successful responses.

Introduction to the Question Types

The *Social Studies: Analytical Essays* test in United States and world history is intended to assess how well a prospective teacher of social studies understands and can communicate some of the enduring issues in American and world history. The test is composed of two constructed-response questions. Each question is interdisciplinary and draws on at least two of the following fields: United States history, world history, government/civics/political science, geography, and economics. Questions may also include material from the behavioral science fields of sociology, anthropology, and psychology.

Each question has two components: subject matter (either United States or world subject matter) and time frame (either historical or contemporary issues). Thus, if one of the two questions concerns United States subject matter and contemporary issues, the other question would concern world subject matter and historical issues. One of the questions incorporates material such as a map, chart, graph, table, cartoon, diagram, quotation, or an excerpt from a document. The emphasis in this question is on bringing outside knowledge to bear on the interpretation of this material. One of the two questions usually contains content reflecting the diverse experiences of people in the United States as related to gender, culture, and/or race, and/or content relating to Latin America, Africa, Asia, or Oceania.

What to Study

Success on this test is not simply a matter of learning more about the structure of constructed-response questions. Cogent organization is important, but success on the test also requires real knowledge of the field. The test evaluates your ability to convey an understanding of some of the significant themes in American and world history. It therefore would serve you well to read books and review notes in these subject areas.

The following books are particularly relevant to the types of knowledge and ability covered by the test. **Note:** The test is not based on these resources, nor do they necessarily cover every topic that may be included in the test.

United States History

Textbooks, especially condensed versions, are the most immediately accessible and useful tools for identifying major themes in American history and organizing them into coherent chronologies. These are two readable texts:

Divine, Robert. *America Past and Present,* brief 4th ed. Vol. I and II. Longman, 1998.

Henretta, James. *America: A Concise History,* 2nd ed. Vol. I and II. Bedford-St. Martin's, 2002.

Also useful are studies that focus on a single issue over an extended period of time. Race, gender, and ethnicity are important themes in contemporary history. The following are helpful introductions:

Evans, Sara. *Born for Liberty.* Free Press, 1987.

This narrative history addresses the main themes in women's history—political, economic, and social—from the colonial era to the present day.

Meier, August, and Elliott Rudwick. *From Plantation to Ghetto,* 3rd ed. Hill and Wang, 1976.

This study, although written a generation ago, remains an authoritative survey of race relations and the African American experience from the era of slavery through the Civil Rights movement.

Takaki, Ronald. *A Different Mirror.* Back Bay, 1993.

Takaki's study looks at the experiences of non-European immigrants—from Mexico, China, and Japan, as well as Africa—from the nineteenth century into the post-Second World War period.

Weeks, Philip. *Farewell, My Nation: The American Indian and the United States in the Nineteenth Century,* 2nd ed. Harlan Davidson, 2001.

Farewell, My Nation describes the phases of federal policies toward Native Americans from early attempts at assimilation through Indian removal, concentration on reservations, Plains wars, and late nineteenth-century land and education reforms.

Exams in American history also focus on the big events. The following are more-penetrating elaborations on subjects found in history textbooks:

Foner, Eric. A *Short History of Reconstruction.* Harper & Row, 1990.

Reconstruction is a recurring exam topic, and Foner's book is a more accessible and abridged version of his *Reconstruction,* currently the definitive work on the era.

Heilbroner, Robert, and Aaron Singer. *The Economic Transformation of America: 1600 to the Present,* 4th ed. Harcourt Brace, 1999.

America's economic history is central to American history. This slim book—by an economic historian of the first order—is useful in all of its chapters, but perhaps especially so in explaining and describing the industrial revolution.

Kennedy, David M. *Freedom from Fear: The American People in Depression and War 1929–1945.* Oxford University Press, 1999.

The Great Depression and the New Deal are two essentials in understanding twentieth-century American history. Kennedy's history is long, but few are as well written. The first half of the book addresses the Depression and the New Deal; the second half, U.S. involvement in the Second World War.

Leuchtenburg, William. *The Perils of Prosperity 1914–1932,* 2nd ed. Chicago, 1993.

This is an eminently readable work by a renowned historian on America's involvement in the First World War, the peace settlement that followed, and the American economy and culture in the 1920s.

Patterson, James T. *Grand Expectations: The United States 1945–1974*. Oxford University Press, 1996.

A lot of test topics cover the post-Second World War period. *Grand Expectations* is an expansive and relatively comprehensive survey of the major issues of that period: the Cold War and Vietnam, race relations and the Civil Rights movement, the feminist movement, postwar affluence, political and social reforms, and the unraveling of America in the 1960s.

Potter, David M. *The Impending Crisis 1848–1861*. Harper, 1976.

Potter's history addresses some of the key themes in nineteenth-century American history: slavery, sectional crisis, the causes of Southern secession, and the outbreak of Civil War. Although very detailed, it remains the best single volume on the subject.

Watson, Harry. *Liberty and Power: The Politics of Jacksonian America*. Hill and Wang, 1990.

Watson's study provides a broad portrait of American society in the "age of Jackson" and then zeroes in on its famed political conflicts as the federal government was adjusting to a rapidly expanding economy.

Wood, Gordon S. *The American Revolution: A History,* Modern Library, 2002.

This is a brief and concise analysis of the standard events and perceptions that led to American independence, wrapped up in the author's influential thesis that the Revolution was profoundly revolutionary.

Understanding What the Questions Are Asking

It is impossible to write a successful response to a question unless you thoroughly understand the question. Often test takers jump into their written response without taking enough time to analyze exactly what the question is asking, how many different parts of the question need to be addressed, and how the information in the accompanying quotes, cartoons, charts, or tables needs to be addressed. The time you invest in making sure you understand what the question is asking will very likely pay off in a better performance, as long as you budget your time and do not spend a large proportion of the available time just reading the question.

Examine the overall question closely, then identify what specific questions are being asked, mentally organize your response, and outline your key themes. But leave yourself plenty of time to write your answer. If you think out your response beforehand, your essay will probably be stronger. But ending an essay with the phrase "Out of time" will win no extra points from the scorers.

Sample Question 1

To illustrate the importance of understanding the question before you begin writing, let's start with a sample question:

"We conclude that in the field of public education the doctrine of *separate but equal* has no place. Separate educational facilities are inherently unequal. Therefore, we hold that the plaintiffs and others similarly situated for whom the actions have been brought are, by reason of the segregation complained of, deprived of the equal protection of the laws guaranteed by the Fourteenth Amendment."

Earl Warren, Chief Justice of the United States Supreme Court
***Brown* v. *Board of Education of Topeka,* 1954**

"We regard the decision of the Supreme Court in the school case [*Brown* v. *Board of Education of Topeka*] as clear abuse of judicial power. It climaxes a trend in the Federal judiciary undertaking to legislate, in derogation of the authority of Congress, and to encroach upon the reserved rights of the states and the people."

Declaration of Ninety-Six Southern Congressmen
March 12, 1956

Using the two excerpts above and your knowledge of twentieth-century United States history and government, write an essay in which you do the following :

A. Describe the legal and social conditions in the United States that generated the *Brown* v. *Board of Education of Topeka* case in 1954.

B. Analyze the conflict of opinions expressed or implied in the two excerpts with specific reference to the concept of "equal protection of the law" and the concept of "reserved rights of the states."

Identifying the key components of the question

- The sample question used in this chapter has two quotes followed by two questions. (These are actually assigned tasks rather than questions, but the actual test always refers to them as "questions.")

- Read each quote carefully and identify its central theme.

- Read each question carefully and determine how the quotes apply to each question.

- Question A: Describe the legal/social conditions that generated *Brown.* Using your knowledge of American history, discuss the history of southern segregation and other forms of racial discrimination.

- Question B: Contrast the message in Quote #1—the Fourteenth Amendment's federal guarantee of equal protection of the law for all, with the message in Quote #2—the federal government may not encroach on rights reserved for states.

- If you have relevant historical knowledge, use it.

Organizing your response

Successful responses start with successful planning, either with an outline or with another form of notes. By planning your response, you greatly decrease the chance that you will forget to answer any part of the question. You increase the chance of creating a well-organized response, which is something the scorers look for. Your note-taking space also gives you a place to jot down thoughts whenever you think of them—for example, when you have an idea about one part of the question while you are writing your response to another part. Like taking time to make sure you understand what the question is asking, planning your response is time well invested, although you must keep track of the time so that you leave sufficient time to write your response.

To illustrate a possible strategy for planning a response, let us focus again on the sample question introduced in the previous section. We analyzed the question and found that it asked for a two-part response. You might begin by jotting down those parts on your notes page, leaving space under each. This will ensure that you address each part when you begin writing.

Sample notes—main parts to be answered

Here you start by identifying each part of the question:

I. Describe:

    A. Legal conditions that led to *Brown v. Board*

    B. Social conditions that led to *Brown v. Board*

II. Contrast conflicting opinions of:

    A. *Brown v. Board*

    B. Southern Declaration

Sample notes—ideas under each main part

You then might quickly fill out the main ideas you want to address in each part, like this:

I. Describe:

    A. Legal conditions that led to *Brown v. Board*

        1. Southern states pass school segregation laws

    B. Social conditions that led to *Brown v. Board*

        1. Unequal, inferior schools for southern African Americans

II. Contrast conflicting opinions of:

A. *Brown v. Board*

    1. Separate but equal has no place because separate schools are inherently unequal

    2. Segregation denies southern Blacks 14th Amendment guarantee of equal protection of law

B. Southern Declaration

    1. *Brown v. Board* is an abuse of judicial power because Supreme Court is in effect passing legislation, a right reserved for Congress

    2. Supreme Court is encroaching on rights reserved for states

To earn the highest number of points from the scorers, you will need to do all of the following:

- Answer all parts of the question.
- Give reasons for your answers.
- Demonstrate subject-specific knowledge in your answer.
- Refer to the data in the stimulus.

Sample notes—added ideas

Now look at your notes and add any ideas that would address these characteristics. Notice the additions that are made below.

This is where you use your knowledge of United States history. What you put here depends on how much you know. The following are some possible responses:

I. Describe:

A. Legal conditions that led to *Brown v. Board*

    1. Southern states pass school segregation laws

    2. Southern states segregate all public facilities (buses, playgrounds, parks, theaters, hospitals, etc.)

        a. Upheld by Supreme Court in *Plessy v. Ferguson* (1896)

3. Related forms of legal discrimination

   a. Disenfranchisement (poll tax, literacy test, property requirement, White primary, grandfather clause)

   b. Absence of federal antilynching law

   c. Vagrancy laws, convict-lease laws, sharecropping are means of racial control

B. Social conditions that led to *Brown v. Board*

   1. Unequal, inferior schools for southern African Americans

      a. High illiteracy rates, few college graduates, few professionals

   2. Denied the vote, southern Blacks have no political recourse for redressing their grievances

   3. Southern Blacks are subjected to violence and intimidation

   4. High rates of poverty, few job/housing opportunities

II. Contrast conflicting opinions of:

A. *Brown v. Board*

   1. Separate but equal has no place because separate schools are inherently unequal

      a. Supreme Courts asserts federal authority to declare state legislation illegal

   2. Segregation denies southern Blacks 14th Amendment guarantee of equal protection of law

      a. Supreme court has the power of judicial review, to declare legislation unconstitutional

      b. Federal and Constitutional law take precedence over state law; state segregation is invalid if it is in violation of the Constitution

B. Southern Declaration

1. *Brown v. Board* is an abuse of judicial power because Supreme Court is in effect passing legislation, a right reserved for Congress

   a. Separation of powers—courts interpret laws; they may not pass or administer legislation

2. Supreme Court is encroaching on rights reserved for states

   a. U.S. is a federalist system—all powers not articulated in Constitution as federal are reserved for states

   b. Public education is a local and state matter; federal government has no legal authority to interfere

You have now created the skeleton of your written response.

Writing your response

Now the important step of writing your response begins. The scorers will not consider your notes when they score your paper, so it is crucial that you integrate all the important ideas from your notes into your actual written response.

Some test takers believe that every written response on a Praxis test has to be in formal essay form—that is, with an introductory paragraph, then paragraphs with the response to the question, then a concluding paragraph. This is the case for very few Praxis tests (e.g., *English* and *Writing*). The *Social Studies: Analytical Essays* test does **not** require formal essays, so you should use techniques that allow you to communicate information efficiently and clearly. For example, you can use bulleted or numbered lists, or a chart, or a combination of essay and chart.

Returning to our sample question, see below how the outline of the response to the first part of the question can become the final written response. What follows is an actual response by a test taker.

Sample response that received a score of 4

A. The legal conditions that generated Brown vs. the Board of Education can be summed up in a series of laws known as the Jim Crow laws. The laws which existed primarily in the Southern U.S. systematically excluded African Americans from full participation in the society. These laws called for separation of the races by creating or designating separate facilities for African Americans and whites. This resulted in segregation in public transport, dining facilities, recreation facilities, schools, jobs, and housing. Likewise their voting rights were limited.

The social conditions surrounding this case were that African Americans were systematically discriminated against in all aspects of life. They were denied decent jobs, fair housing, good educations, and full participation in government. Thus resulting in 2 societies—one oppressing the other.

B. In striking down the separate but equal doctrine the Supreme Court was exercising it's right to declare any state law unconstitutional as established in Fletcher v. Peck. In striking down this law the Supreme Court was acting in the interests of the nation in guaranteeing all its citizens equal protection before the law. That is to be treated the same as any other citizen and to not be singled out, when dealing with the law. Blacks could not be treated differently than Whites before the law. So the Supreme Court acted within it's rights in striking this law down.

The opposing side argues from a point of view which recalls that any right not specifically preserved for the federal government, was to belong to the state, as written in the constitution. State education is strictly a local and state issue, the 96 Southern Congressman argue that the court overstepped its bounds in declaring this law unconstitutional. Likewise they believe that in striking down this law the Supreme Court is in effect "legislating" a right reserved for the congress, president, and state assemblies. Thus not only is the Supreme Court interfering in local affairs but encroaching on the legislative and executive branches right to pass laws.

Commentary on sample response that earned a score of 4

This essay is particularly strong on Part B. Although *Fletcher* v. *Peck* is misidentified (it should be *Marbury* v. *Madison*), the test taker states clearly the conflict between federal government—which can declare state laws unconstitutional—and states' rights. The writer explains the argument from the Declaration of 96 Southern Congressmen that state education is a local and state affair and consequently that the federal government had no authority to rule on the matter. Part A is adequate but needs a bit more historical development.

Sample response that received a score of 2

Upon the conclusion of the Civil War of the United States, Abraham Lincoln issued his Emancipation Proclamation. This would free the Negro slaves of their masters in the United States but all in all left them with little freedom and little if any rights. Negroes were mostly going back to slavery in the South because they were kept from getting care and food from Southerners if they didn't work for it.

In time Congress would pass the 1st Civil Rights Act to protect and offer a better life for Negroes in America. Although Congress would be opposed by President Andrew Johnson and later by many other leaders, Blacks were able to unite and form a solid group to fight for their rights.

As the 1950's approached the United States found itself in the position of world leader of freedom and democracy. If this was so how could they discriminate against Negroes, of course they would have no credibility if they did. Also how would other nations feel in assisting the U.S. against communism if they knew the U.S. discriminated against it's own people? In turn, the U.S. had a practice which was referred to as "Separate but equal." Blacks would have all Whites did but it would be separate. Separate Rest Rooms, Restaurants, etc. This segregation was particularly evident in the Southern region of the country.

On the topic of schools for children, it was designed that separate but equal be enforced. But it was only partially enforced. Whites had all the advantages and Blacks had poor schools. As often follows a bad situation, Blacks began to protest and complain about this mistreatment and fought for desegregation. In 1954 the Supreme Court ruled that separate but equal was not Constitutional, and to be done with. In which desegregation took place and Blacks were given a fair chance in American schools.

Commentary on sample response that earned a score of 2

The historical information in Part A is extremely vague and undeveloped. However, more development of Part A wouldn't raise the score because the writer of this essay doesn't address Part B. The Supreme Court decision is identified as declaring school segregation unconstitutional, but the issue of federal authority *versus* states' rights is not identified and the Declaration of 96 Southern Congressmen is not acknowledged. As a general rule, it is essential that test takers address each component of a question.

In conclusion

Whatever format you select, the important thing is that your answer be thorough, complete, and detailed. You need to be certain that you do the following:

- Answer all parts of the question.
- Give reasons for your answers.
- Demonstrate subject-specific knowledge in your answer.
- Refer to the data in the stimulus.

Chapter 5
Practice Test—*Social Studies: Analytical Essays*

▶ ▶ ▶ ▶ ▶ ▶ ▶ ▶ ▶ ▶ ▶ ▶

Now that you have worked through strategies and preparation relating to the *Social Studies: Analytical Essays* test, you should take the following practice test. This test is an actual Praxis test, now retired. You will probably find it helpful to simulate actual testing conditions, giving yourself 60 minutes to work on the questions. You can use the lined answer pages provided if you wish.

Keep in mind that the test you take at an actual administration will have different questions. You should not expect your level of performance to be exactly the same as when you take the test at an actual administration, since numerous factors affect a person's performance in any given testing situation.

When you have finished the practice questions, you can read through the sample responses with scorer annotations in chapter 6.

THE **PRAXIS**
S E R I E S
Professional Assessments for Beginning Teachers ®

TEST NAME:

Social Studies:

Analytical Essays (0082)

Time—60 minutes

2 Questions

Question 1

The United States emerged victorious from both the First World War and the Second World War. Using your knowledge of United States history during the two postwar decades, 1918–1928 and 1945–1955, write an essay in which you describe and analyze

A. one or two major similarities between these two decades

   AND

B. one or two major differences between these two decades.

Support your essay with specific historical examples.

NOTES

Question 2

WORLD ENERGY DEMAND

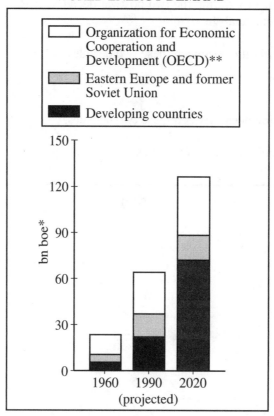

WORLD ENERGY SUPPLY, BY TYPE

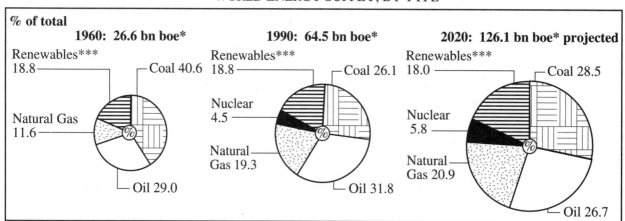

*   bn boe = billion barrels of oil or oil equivalent
**   OECD members are 24 of the wealthiest, most industrialized countries in the world.
*** Renewable energy sources include wind, hydro, solar, and wood.

The bar graph and the pie charts on the facing page illustrate world energy demand and world energy supply by type for the years 1960, 1990, and 2020 (projected). Using this information and your knowledge of economics, geography, history, and politics, write an essay in which you do the following.

A. In two or three sentences, summarize the trends in world energy demand <u>and</u> world energy supply.

B. Identify and discuss the impact these trends are likely to have in the near future on the world economy, the world environment, and world politics. Use specific examples to support your arguments.

NOTES

Begin your response to Question 1 here.

(Question 1—*Continued*)

(Question 1—*Continued*)

(Question 1—*Continued*)

(Question 1—*Continued*)

Begin your response to Question 2 here.

(Question 2—*Continued*)

(Question 2—*Continued*)

(Question 2—*Continued*)

(Question 2—*Continued*)

Chapter 6
Samples Responses and How They Were Scored—
Social Studies: Analytical Essays

▶ ▶ ▶ ▶ ▶ ▶ ▶ ▶ ▶ ▶ ▶ ▶

This chapter presents actual sample responses to the questions on the practice test and explanations for the scores they received. As discussed in chapter 3, each question on the *Social Studies: Analytical Essays* test is scored on a scale from 0 to 5. The General Scoring Guide used to score these parts is reprinted here for your convenience.

Score	Comment

5
- Provides a full, insightful analysis, with logical, well-supported explanations and conclusions
- Interprets the stimulus (if applicable) accurately and applies it effectively
- Demonstrates a superior understanding of the subject, including interdisciplinary connections
- Provides well-chosen and accurate factual information
- Is well organized and very clear throughout

4
- Provides a substantial analysis, with logically developed explanations and conclusions
- Interprets the stimulus (if applicable) accurately and applies it appropriately
- Demonstrates a strong understanding of the subject
- Provides relevant and accurate factual information, with very few significant errors
- Is organized and clear

3
- Provides an analysis with generally logical explanations and conclusions
- Interprets and applies the stimulus (if applicable) in a mostly accurate and appropriate way
- Demonstrates an adequate understanding of the subject
- Provides mostly relevant and accurate factual information (may have a few significant errors)
- Is, for the most part, organized and clear

2
- Provides a limited analysis, with poorly developed explanations and conclusions
- Interprets and applies the stimulus (if applicable) with a lack of accuracy and appropriateness
- Demonstrates a limited understanding of the subject
- Lacks relevant and accurate factual information (may have significant errors)
- May be poorly organized or lack clarity

1
- Provides scarcely any analysis, logical explanations, or conclusions
- Misinterprets the stimulus (if applicable) and applies it inappropriately
- Demonstrates very little understanding of the subject
- Provides scarcely any relevant or accurate information (may have many significant errors)
- May be disorganized or confusing

0
- Completely inaccurate or inappropriate, blank, off topic, or only a restatement of the prompt

Question 1

We will now look at five responses to Question 1 and see how the scoring guide above was used to rate each response.

Sample response that earned a score of 5

Despite victory in both wars, the post-war periods exhibited many more significant differences than similarities. The similarities were more superficial than substantive. First, in both periods the U.S. aspires to provide moral leadership through a world organization. Wilson's 14 points and plan for the leagues of nations was nurtured after world war II by the Bretton Woods accords on currency and the formation of the U.N. Secondly, both wars provided a demographic boost which stimulated the economy and provided new consumer goods, in the 20's cars and refrigerators. In the late 40's homes, cars, and household goods for veterans. The American family changed irrevocably in the 20's, the era to which researchers ascribe a new sexual freedom due to the automobile. Many of the sexual practices considered characteristics of modern industrial societies became dominant in the twenties and were common in the late 40's, when women had jobs and autonomy.

Yet, on serious appraisal, the differences were more significant. In the first place, the U.S. retired into isolationism, limited immigration, and didn't participate in the League of Nations in the 20's. After WW II by contrast, we forwarded and supported the U.N., in crucial military, cultural, and economic presence work with and imposed the Pax Americana, picking up police functions as the British and French wound down their empires. Secondly, the GI Bill and loans for veterans subsidized a new middle-class so that growth, while slow, was steady and provided a base for even growth, unlike the pattern of the 20's where farmers had been excluded from prosperity. Thirdly, the ideology of "freedom" enunciated in Roosevelt's speeches led to quiet slow progress in race relations through legal victories and Truman's desegregation of the Army. Returning veterans founded Mexican-American pressure groups as well. Thus the decade 1945-55 produced many economic and social changes which would lead to the ferment of the sixties. The principal exceptions to the progressive victories of the late 40's and early 50's was the retrograde social policy about women. In the twenties women had gotten the vote, forged their political party and had spirited public leaders like Jane Addams, Amelia Earheart, and Parker Sibley. In the decade following WW II, women (with notable exceptions like Clare Booth Luce and

Sample Responses to Question 1, continued

Margaret Chase Smith) did not weild political power. Returning men got the jobs held by Rosie the Riveter and a converted public opinion emphasized domesticity, consumerism, and child bearing.

More significant than either the similarities or differences noted above was the unique role played by American technology in the decade following WW II. As the unique (for a while) possessors of the atom bomb and the developers of modern data processing and electronics, we built with substantial state investment an economy which was strong in invention, in manufacturing, in education, and in services. Despite the common notion of the Eisenhower years as dull, they brought us the interstate highway system, a significant (if brief) improvement in public education and a sense of pride. While the twenties had been a decade of speculation and easy money, the decade after WW II produced infrastructures for both world and interstate commerce, strength and stabilized a broad middle class, and created a momentary (if illusory) sense that "meritocracy" and "technocracy" would allow us to go beyond the mistakes of the past.

Scoring Commentary

- For a response to earn a 5, the test taker needs to analyze at least one significant similarity and one difference between the two periods and support its arguments with substantial relevant information from both decades. The test taker should display a superior understanding of the material.

- This essay begins with a thesis statement (that the differences are more important than similarities).

- Then the test taker discusses multiple similarities and multiple differences between the two decades.

- Similarities: an attempt at multinationalism (with the creation of the League of Nations and then the United Nations); a thriving consumer economy; more permissive sexual values (which were somewhat new to the 1920s and common in the late 1940s); new technologies after both wars (cars and refrigerators after the First World War; the atomic bomb, data processing, and electronics after the Second).

- Differences: the U.S. became isolationist after the First World War and internationalist after the Second (imposing a "Pax Americana"); the women's rights movement culminated with suffrage after the First World War, whereas there was a return to domesticity after the Second.

- There is also a contrast between the post-First World War speculative economy and the post-Second World War stabilized economy; this is mostly just confusing but is of little consequence in the context of the whole essay.

- The test taker assigns some additional correct and appropriate characteristics to the post-First World War period—limited immigration, farmers were excluded from prosperity—and to the post-Second World War period—changing race relations, the GI Bill, the interstate highway system. Although no contrasts are made here, the essay does demonstrate broad knowledge of the time periods.

- This essay has best-choice examples which are well developed, and there is more than enough relevant information.

Sample response that earned a score of 4

The two post-war decades, 1918-1928 and 1945-1955 have some deceptive similarities. The United States attempted a Leadership Role in both, though less successfully in the First period than in the second. The establishment of the Leauge of Nations following the 'Great War' (with the hope of avoiding a second) and the creation of the United Nations (again to promote peace) is one example. For the United States both post war periods saw a "BOOM". The High-living 20's and The Happy days of the 50's and a general - Reaffirmation of American ideals.

However the similarities between the two periods are overshadowed by the often subtle but telling differences. After the First world war the United states retreated, despite president Wilson's efforts into isolationism, the Leauge of Nations succeeded less in promoting peace than in simply letting the stage for another war. The creation of Artificial Nation states and Boundaries, The isolation of the defeated powers, and the Constitution of military alliances illustrate this point. In contrast the 1945 - 1955 period saw the United States accepting a position of world leadership wholeheartedly, abandoning isolationism as unrealistic and unsafe. Truman's support for Democratic Nations battling insurgency, the Marshall Plan for the re-building of Europe, the fair and far sighted treatment of Germany and Japan, are all major differences from 1918-1928. While 1918-1928 saw the failure of that generation's dreams and the decay into aggression and inevitable war (Facism in Italy, Imperialism in Japan, and Free-Kores/Nazi movement of Germany) the 1945-1955 period suffered only a 'cold war'; with Democratic growth in the former enemy nations. The Soviet Union, having successfully created a 'Buffer Zone' in the Warsaw pact, avoided direct confrontation with the West and another Global war, a very sharp contrast to the instable alliances that actually precipitated the war of 1914-1918.

Scoring Commentary

- In a response that earns a 4, the test taker needs to analyze at least one significant similarity and one difference between the two periods and support its arguments with some relevant factual information, although the treatment may be imbalanced. A strong understanding of the material should be displayed.

- In this essay, the test taker discusses two similarities (the United States' attempted role in world leadership with the League of Nations and United Nations, economic prosperity) and one difference (isolationism *versus* internationalism) between the two decades.

- There is imbalance in this essay. The two similarities are correctly identified, but only very briefly discussed. The discussion of the one difference, however, is very strong—well-organized, integrated, and detailed.

Sample Responses to Question 1, continued

- This test taker characterizes the isolationism of the interwar period and the internationalism following the Second World War. The consequences of each policy are shown and the two periods are tied together by a demonstration of how the isolationist policies of the former period made a necessity of the internationalist policies of the latter period.

- This essay contains strong specific knowledge of the period: failure of the League and treatment of defeated powers helped to create the rise of fascism and nazism in Europe and militarism in Japan, which set the stage for another war. Consequently, in order to avoid yet another war, the Marshall Plan was used, Germany and Japan were rebuilt, democracy took root in former enemy nations, the Soviet Union created a buffer zone with the Warsaw Pact, and a Cold War substituted for direct military confrontation.

- The imbalanced treatment of similarities and differences keeps this essay from the rating of 5, but its overall strength lifts it above a 3. We score holistically, and the discussion of the difference is exceptional.

- This essay is relatively brief, but it is focused and to the point. It doesn't waste words.

Sample response that earned a score of 3

The decades following World War One and World War Two are interesting comparison studies. Both periods were remarkably similar in the Economic prosperity that flourished during the periods after war, Americans felt great pride in their country and culture following these great victories. They were tremendous periods of hope and celebration and Americans were sure of their Cultural Superiority. They also were fairly conservative times (prohibition) and times with relatively little social unrest. Americans were united under a common goal that is now hardly imaginable given the demonstrations surrounding the Vietnam War.

There are, however, differences between the decade after WW I and WW II. The major difference surrounds the foreign policies of the time. Isolationism was Americas response to WW I. The American public wanted little to do with foreign affairs. The less we were burdened by other countries the better. Woodrow Wilson was alone in his belief that a battered Germany needed our help or war would again rear its ugly head.

Wilson's strong opinions on how to treat war torn Germany came to him because he was a 9 year old Southerner after the Civil War. He saw the devastation caused by war and was sympathetic to the losers. To kick people when they are down creates an environment that breeds dictatorship, communism and other threats to democracy. Wilson, however, died before he could convince the American people of this.

The American people truly ran the politics of the 20's. The presidents all tended to go along with popular thought and the idea at this time was celebration of all things American. Ford put a car within economic reach of every family, the stock market was a way to get rich quick and Economic prosperity led Americans to believe they were better on their own. America was isolated and would soon come to suffer for it.

The 50's were likewise care free. The American economy prospered and pride in the country flourished. Instead of Ford putting a car in every garage, Elvis put Rock and Roll in every radio. TV, music and most of popular culture was dominated by all things American, just as it had been in the 20's. Like the revolutionary bob haircut of the 20's dominated fashion so did new American fashion ideas like Bobbie socks and sadle shoes take over fashion.

Eisenhower was quick to notice that history repeats itself and kept American deeply tied up in foreign policy. Korea was invaded and communism was counteracted upon at any cost. Americans had learned their lesson and relied on government to keep a firm hold upon democracy. They also relied on government to curtail the ravenous spending that brought about the huge stock market Crash of '29. The limits on creditors and bank investments made the prosperity of post-WWI American much more stable.

The two decades were similar in spirit. Americans were proud of America and their culture. The country was victorious and prosperous. The main differences lie in the foreign policies of the two decades.

Scoring Commentary

- A response that earns a 3 will have a mostly accurate but general description of the two periods. It may discuss primarily one decade or focus primarily on differences or similarities. It may contain significant errors.

- Essays that earn a 3 tend to be less analytically focused, being more a narrative or listing of events of the period. The information tends to be far more general. Or such essays may contain significant errors that lower the overall score.

- This test taker correctly identifies a similarity between the two periods (prosperity), but with no development, and a difference (isolationism versus internationalism) with some development (Wilson's foresight; Eisenhower and anticommunism; the point on Korea is a bit confusing). There is no mention of the League of Nations or the United Nations.

- There are two significant errors: this test taker implies that prohibition marked both decades (it did not), and states that the Eisenhower administration limited spending, credit, and bank investments (it definitely did not).

- This essay tends toward glittering generalities that obscure rather than clarify its points—Americans felt *great pride,* there was *hope* and *celebration,* and people *truly ran* politics in the '20s. This is common in responses that earn a 3.

Sample Responses to Question 1, continued

- This essay also tends to speak in period stereotypes rather than analytical observations: the '20s as a get-rich-quick, car-in-every-garage, women-in-bobbed-haircuts era; people in the '50s wearing bobby socks and saddle shoes as they listened to Elvis. These are not incorrect, but these are overstated caricatures rather than best-choice examples.

- When the strengths of this essay are weighed against the imbalanced treatment and errors, it should be considered adequate, but not more than adequate.

Sample response that earned a score of 2

There appears to be little disagreement among historians over the belief that America in the past world war decades can be characterized as being peaceful and prosperous. Overall, there was political, economic, and social stability that followed in the immediate decades following World War I and World War II. The 1920's were "roaring" and the 1950's had an "affluent society." Although historical parallels and similarities can be drawn between the economic and social forces of the two periods, some social forces were not in synch, e.g. the role of women in the work force and family.

The first major similarity between the years 1918-28 and 1945-55 are economic in nature. America was, for the first time, a major world country with awesome economic and trading capacity. After the wars, most other powerful countries were left devastated financially. America was relatively well. The allied and defeated countries were dependent on America to nurture their economies back to health. This in turn left our economy booming. Our employment, productivity, and standards of living rose significantly as taxes were law and stable.

Related to economics are the political philosophies of the two periods. Isolationism characterized the two decades. This is mostly due to the fact that Americas didn't want to get involved in any global conflicts after they had experienced the horrific world wars. Americans shunned worldly affairs and even tended to stick to the same Republican "laissez-faire" philosophy Presidents (Harding and Eisenhower). Both Presidents had the focus on America and preferred to shy away from international affairs and concentrate on rebuilding American interests with intense patriotic fervor.

One of the major differences that can be seen between these two periods is with women's role in the family. Some women worked outside of the family during World War I, but there were many more "Rosie the Riveters" during the second world war. After the first world war, women were still unable to vote and their "place" was still felt to be overwhelmingly in the home with their husband and family. After the second world war, women had the right to vote and were much more experienced at being in the workplace, taking care of their families without a husband. Women were much less likely to quit their jobs and run back home in 1945. Betty Friedan's The Feminism Mystique came out in 1947 and women started taking control of families and demanding a more equal partnership in the marriage.

The same balancing act happened in the workplace as well. Women stayed in permanent type jobs, expanded their diversity in the workforce, and attempted to manage jobs and family together. Family was still important, but so was the ability to work and be a breadwinner. After all, the actress who played June Cleaver on Leave it to the Beaver was a working mother herself.

Women are still trying to lead dichotomous lives today. The struggle continues. We are still a very prosperous nation and families are important, but the effects that the world wars had on American forever put in motion the wheels of change.

Scoring Commentary

- A response that earns a 2 will be vague and/or limited in its understanding, limited in its analysis, and weak in its knowledge. It often contains major errors.

- This essay contains enough correct information to lift it above a score of 1, but it is too overwhelmed by misinformation and misunderstanding to be an adequate response.

- A similarity between the two periods (prosperity) is correctly identified. The test taker understands that Harding and Eisenhower were the respective presidents and that women entered the workforce in larger numbers after the Second World War. But that's about as far as it goes.

- Otherwise, this essay is wrong in ways great and small: the writer argues that both periods were characterized by isolationism, a fatal flaw in itself. It argues that the U.S. became an important economic power for the first time after the First World War, and that women could not vote at that time. The test taker also seems to place the beginnings of the feminist movement in the 1945–55 period, first by misdating the publication of Betty Friedan's *Feminine Mystique* to 1947. (It came almost a generation later in 1963.)

- There is more understanding in this essay than in an essay that earns a 1, but its flaws outweigh its few strengths.

Sample response that earned a score of 1

World War I and II had very similar distinctive qualities or assets during their eras. For example, during World W I and II the official foreign policy for the United States was isolationism. The United States did not believe in involving itself with international crisis. The United States during these time periods still had racial polyerization and segregated laws in their society.

Sample Responses to Question 1, continued

The military remained segregated during these time periods, and much of the south was separated by color lines.

The major difference between these eras are also well noted. For example, During World War I the United States economy was very good. Business enterprises were booming and the infrastructure of the U.S. was very good. However, during the time period of World War II, the United States economy was very bad. The Great depression was occuring and our nation was battling major social crises such as homelessness, bankruptcy, foreclosures, and hunger crises.

Another difference, noted concerning these eras was prohibition. During the period of World War I, alcohol was not allowed. The distribution, transportation, and manufacturing of alcohol was illegal. On the contrary, during World War II the United States repealed prohibition and legalized the production and sell of alcohol.

Scoring Commentary

- A response that earns a 1 misunderstands the question, and/or contains little or no useful information, and/or has massive errors.

- There is some correct information in this essay, and it is clearly organized, but it earns a 1 quite simply because the time frame is missed. There is a discussion of the wartime periods rather than the postwar decades, The test taker argues that *during* the First World War (rather than after), the U.S. was isolationist (hardly), that *during* the war the military was segregated, that the economy was good, and that alcohol was prohibited. Also incorrect, there is an argument (showing evidence of profound misunderstanding) that *during* the Second World War the economy was bad because *during* the war the Great Depression was raging.

Question 2

We will now look at five responses to Question 2 to see how the scoring guide was used.

Sample response that earned a score of 5

World energy demand between the years 1960 to 2020 (projected) show consistent increase in worldwide demand, approximately doubling every 30 years. The percentage of proportion of demand by developing countries changes significantly over this time period, with an increase 3 - 4 times previous demand within the 30 year time period. World energy supply appears to be relatively consistent with demand, again showing an approximate tripling of supply every approximate 30 years, as indicated by the pie chart.

These significant increases in supply and demand for the world's energy sources will have definite impact on the world economy, the world environment and world politics. The following discussion will detail some of these effects, using examples from history and current affairs that have already demonstrated such effects.

A significant factor affecting the distribution of energy supply to the world is the geographic location of various energy sources. For example, much of the available world oil is found in the Persian Gulf, and this has dramatically shaped the politics, international relations, and economy of this region and the many countries who are dependent on Persian Gulf oil.

The United States, Russia, and other industrialized countries of the world, including Europe, rely heavily on oil available from the Persian Gulf. This continues to give these countries, such as Iran, Iraq, Kuwait, and Saudi Arabia, political power in the world and certainly fuels their economies, Militarily, the U.S. has realized its dependence on the Middle East and has sought goals to develop alternative sources of energy, to avoid the high cost and risk of being dependent on an area of the world that has proven to be unpredictable and risky in its political policies. Indeed, previous oil embargos and raising the cost of crude oil have significantly impacted the price of gasoline in the developed nations of the world, which in turn fuels inflation as transportation costs travel to all areas of the economy. Indeed the U.S. involvement in the Gulf War is directly related to our interests to protect our oil supply, as was it of the allies who similarly join forces

The energy crisis of the 1970s spurred much debate about the use of fossil fuels and the need to develop alternative sources of energy, both to meet future energy need, and to rely less on other nations do supply that need. Fossil fuels, oil, coal, natural gas provide much more pollution then

Sample Responses to Question 2, continued

many renewable energy sources, such as wind, hydro and solar. Judging from the data given in the pie charts the use of fossil fuels in the near future will not decline, in fact, it will remain relatively constant, with some variation in the supply of gas, coal, and oil. This means that in the near future the world will continue to have to deal with environmental problems from heavy dependence on fossil fuels. Coal pollutes the air, as does using gasoline. One effect we are experiencing from car pollution is the effect on ozone - a gas which is poisonous to humans. Mining of coal also greatly affects local economies and private health. Many coal workers experience exposure to coal dust resulting in black lung disease. Mines create boom towns, which become desolate when the mines are closed.

Unfortunately, the harnessing of environmentally friendly energy sources requires more money and technology than the use of fossil fuels, hence third world countries are likely to be more dependent on fossil fuels which will adversely affect their environments and others' through acid rain. Also unfortunate is the slow progress the world has made in converting to renewable energy sources, which with the exception of burning wood, do not cause the pollution and risks of fossil fuels and nuclear energy.

Nuclear energy, while slightly increasing in the total percentage picture, has not been developed, especially in the US as much as was initially thought. The scare with Three Mile Island during the Carter years showed the risks to children and civilians which will occur in using nuclear power. The lessons of Chernobyl and the inability of other countries to control the risks from nuclear fallout to their countries is indeed and will continue to be of grave international concern.

Oil spills in the oceans and the vast resourses to clean up spills is a high cost the world must pay for heavy oil dependence. Developing nations in many parts of the world will not be able to meet their energy needs due to poor economics and poorer technology to develop and clean up after the energy sources our world is dependent upon.

Scoring Commentary

- The question contains two parts, so this commentary breaks down the test taker's essay into its two component parts and evaluates each part separately.

- Part A consists of correctly interpreting the charts. To earn a 5, the essay writer must note increasing energy demand and supply and that the largest demand will come from developing nations, and must say something about proportional energy supplies.

- This test taker does all four things. The writer notes in the first paragraph an increase in demand, particularly in developing nations, and that supply will be consistent with demand. Later it is noted that fossil fuel supply and demand will remain relatively constant, with some variation in gas, coal, and oil. Later still, the test taker mentions that nuclear energy supply and demand will increase slightly.

- For Part B (which is more important than Part A—it tests knowledge rather than ability to read a chart), the test taker must discuss the impact of the energy situation on three areas—the world economy, environment, and politics—and display a superior understanding of these issues.

- This essay contains a discussion of all three things.

- On political impact, this test taker discusses the Persian Gulf, mentioning some of the countries by name. It is pointed out that the dependence of industrialized nations on oil has enhanced the political power of Iran, Iraq, Kuwait, and Saudi Arabia; that the Middle East is unpredictable and risky; and that the U.S. went to war in the Gulf to stabilize the oil supply there.

- On economic impact, the writer points to past oil embargoes, which impact prices, contribute to inflation, and in the 1970s created an energy crisis and fed a drive to find alternative fuel supplies.

- On environmental impact, this essay contains a discussion of pollution from coal and gasoline (and black-lung disease from coal mining), plus impact on the ozone layer (although it doesn't identify what the effect is). The writer also notes the dangers of nuclear energy, using Three Mile Island and Chernobyl as examples, and the problem of nuclear fallout. Also noted are the problem of oil spills and the high cost of cleanup.

Sample response that earned a score of 4

According to the charts, world energy demand from 1960 to 2020 will experience a four-fold growth from just under 30 bn boe to 120 bn boe. Concurrently, the world energy supply will increase from 26.6 bn boe to 126.1 bn boe. More specifically, demand by developing countries will experience the largest growth, followed 2nd by OECD or the most industrialized countries, and 3rd by Eastern European and former Soviet Union countries, whose demand between 1990 and 2020 will actually remain fairly constant. On the supply side, the supply of coal will become a lesser percentage of the total world supply, whereas nuclear energy and natural gas will be used more in 2020 than in 1990.

The total increased demand impacts negatively on the world environment when one considers that the greater the demand, the more resources will be used causing further depletion of nonrenewable resources like coal and oil. That the supply and reliance will be less on coal and more on energy sources like natural gas and nuclear energy is a hopeful sign for energy conservation. However, natural gas like oil and coal is also a nonrenewable energy source. Moreover, like the burning of coal and oil, both the use of geothermal and nuclear energy can result in undesirable social consequences like radiation contamination in the case of nuclear energy.

Sample Responses to Question 2, continued

> The uneven demand, where less developed countries will require more of the supply of the world's energy, on the political scene will continue to cause tensions between traditionally "First" and "Third" World countries. These tensions will become even more problematic when environmental concerns that are lobbied for by individuals and environmental groups are imposed upon developing countries whose main concern is to modernize and develop their industries.
>
> As for the world economy, that developing countries are experiencing such a growth in demand suggests that the developing countries may be undergoing processes of industrialization, modernization, and urbanization. With these processes come the movement of peoples, the development of jobs, and the growth of cities. On the other side, in industrialized countries, processes of deindustrialization can be posited suggesting the problems of social decay, movement of jobs away from cities.

Scoring Commentary

- For Part A, the writer of this essay does everything the question asks: the test taker notes in the first paragraph that demand will increase, as will supply; that most of the demand will come from developing countries; and that coal will decline as a percentage of total energy supply as the importance of nuclear energy and natural gas increases.

- For Part B, the test taker must discuss consequences in at least two areas (politics, economics, and environment) and display a strong understanding of the issues.

- For Part B, this essay is stronger on politics and economics than on environment. Moreover, the points are strong, but there is less specific information here than in the essay that earned a 5.

- On environment, this essay points to the depletion of nonrenewable resources but there is no explanation of how this is an environmental hazard. (Actually, this is more of an economic argument.) Radiation contamination from nuclear energy is identified as a potential hazard, but the idea is not developed.

- On political impact, there is a discussion of potential conflict between industrialized nations, where influential environmentalist lobbies stress energy conservation, and developing nations that need ever-larger amounts of energy to fuel industrialization and modernization.

- This theme on economic impact is continued in the essay: Growing energy demand among developing nations provides them some of the means for economic growth; it allows them to industrialize, which means jobs and growth of cities.

- For Part B, all three areas are addressed, but there is an imbalance of treatment, enough to keep this essay out of the top range.

Sample response that earned a score of 3

The bar graph clearly indicates a profound rise in energy demands over the 60 years projection. The greatest increases in demand are and will continue among the developing countries (i.e., Brazil, Columbia, Laos, Vietnam, etc.). The supply of energy, as demonstrated by the pie charts, has been and will continue to address the rising demands with increasing output.

The pie chart of energy supply indicate an alarmingly small percentage (18.8-18.0%) of renewable energy sources being used. Granted, the 18.0% of 126.1 bn boe is an increase over 18.8% of 26.6; nevertheless, the enormous rise in non-renewables means potentially catastrophic industrial problems by the end of the 21st century. The advent of Nuclear power has provided some relief, but it also carries some real concerns. (i.e. the Chernoble incident and disposing of waste).

With the increased demands being made by developing nations will also come their increasing influence on the politics and economies of the OECD. It is conceivable, if the developing nations can retain control of their own resources, that they may prove to be the dominant political and economic forces of the mid and late 21st century.

The continents of Africa and S. America constitute enormous land masses of only slightly tapped natural resources. Nations such as Kenya, Nigeria, and Zimbabwa, therefore, could prove critical at some future date for their reserves. Other nations, such as Brazil and Madagascar, are depleting one of their resources (the rainforests) and are making little or no effort to replenish the resource.

In conclusion, if the world fails to extend use of more renewable resources and further replenish and protect those we have, the world will turn upside down. The wealthiest nations could become the poorest. The developing ones could become the richest; but in the end, we might all end up on a lifeless rock.

Scoring Commentary

- For Part A, the writer of this essay does everything the question asks. In the first paragraph, the test taker notes rising demand, particularly in developing countries, and rising supply. In the second paragraph, the proportional distribution of fuel supplies is recognized by noting a change in the percentage of nonrenewable energy sources over time and also the advent of nuclear energy.

- For Part B, the test taker must discuss consequences in at least one of the three areas (politics, economics, and environment) and display an adequate understanding of the issues. It is in Part B that the quality of the essay drops.

Sample Responses to Question 2, continued

- On environmental impact, the writer notes the example of Chernobyl, the problem of disposing of nuclear waste, and the depletion of Brazil's and Madagascar's rain forests.

- On politics and economics, the test taker argues that developing nations will become more influential in the future, but the explanation is confusing. Had the writer said that developing nations with reserves of energy would become more influential, or that in consuming more energy, developing nations were becoming industrialized, that would make sense. Instead the connection isn't explained and then the writer branches into discussion of countries with unspecified natural resources.

- The writer then makes the unwarranted statement that the wealthiest nations may become the poorest, and the developing ones the richest.

- Environmental impact is addressed in this essay, but it has only the beginning of a response for politics and economics, combined with some irrelevant and puzzling information.

Sample response that earned a score of 2

In studying the pie chart and bar graph, I have noticed that the demand for energy has been increasing more so for the developing countries. In the world energy supply, the trend seems to be that nuclear energy and natural gas will increasing in terms of supply.

When looking at the bar graph, I have stated above that there is more demand in developing countries for energy. The trend is that energy demand is increasing for everyone. Although when looking at the graph, one can conclude that the most industrialized nations still demand more energy than anyone else. One reason for this are the advances that they have made in technology which require the uses of such energy as nuclear, wind, hydro, and solar.

The impact that this trend will have in the world economy is that only those nations who are economically well off will be able to afford such energy once the demand is increasing everywhere. According to a basic law of economics, when demand is high, it leads to the scarcity of supply, which in turn causes inflation and thus leads the prices to rise. As a result, only those nations will be capable of supplying energy, who are capable of affording it.

In looking at the world energy supply charts, the trend as I mentioned above was more towards nuclear and natural gas. It seems evidence that the impact will be on what types of energy become more supplied than the others. For example, the supply of nuclear energy seems to be increasing, according to the pie chart.

The question that I have is that what affects will this type of energy have on the world environment, and of course, the habitants of this global society? I fear that this type energy seems to be increasing for it maybe a very practical form of energy but imagine the dangers it may have as affects. Imagine the dangers it may cause our natural environment. Once again, the world's most powerful nations will make a decision for the rest of the world. Overall, as I see it, the demands for energy has increased as well as the supply, due to the advancement of society and the technology that we have created to make this world function as well as we can.

Scoring Commentary

- For Part A, the test taker does everything the question asks. The writer notes, in order, that energy demand is increasing faster for developing countries, that there is greater use of nuclear energy and natural gas, and that demand is increasing for everyone. In the final paragraph, the test taker notes an increase in energy supply.

- This essay earns a 2 because in Part B, the test taker attempts a discussion of consequences but is vague and displays only a limited understanding of the issues.

- For Part B, the writer makes no attempt to address political impact.

- On economics, this test taker makes a couple of nonsensical statements: that only well-off nations will be able to afford energy, and that only those nations that can afford energy will be able to supply energy (or perhaps that only nations that supply energy will be able to afford it). It is noted that scarcity of supply causes inflation, but the chart shows no scarcity of supply.

- On environmental impact, the test taker asks what consequences nuclear energy will have on world environment and expresses fear of dangerous effects, but no consequences are identified.

Sample response that earned a score of 1

With industrialization reaching more and more countries and people throughout the world, the demands on world energy supplies are stretched and pushed to the limit. More people and are driving cars more roads and paved and more lights are being used. Existing supplies of energy, like oil for example, are being used in record number. The trend in recent decades has been not only to search for more supplies of energy, like oil, but also to uncover different sources of valuable energy. Solar energy, alternative fuels are just a two of the many new sources on the test block.

The world economy depends greatly on the oil that comes from the Middle East and the OPEC nations. The countrys that control this oil virtually

Sample Responses to Question 2, continued

Scoring Commentary

- For part A, this writer note an increase in energy demand, with supplies "being used in record number[s]." Solar energy is mentioned an alternative energy source, but there is no statement of its significance as a percentage of supply. More importantly, the test taker misinterprets the graph by asserting that demands on world energy supplies are being pushed to the limit. The chart clearly shows supply growing alongside demand.

- In any case, it does not matter how well the test taker handles the first part, because Part B is not answered. There is no attempt in the essay to discuss political or environmental consequences. With regard to economics, the test taker notes that the world is dependent on OPEC oil, but does not identify any consequences.

- The question-specific scoring guide states that essays with "little or no discussion" for Part B earn a score of 1.

Chapter 7
Preparing for the *Social Studies: Interpretation of Materials* Test

▶   ▶   ▶   ▶   ▶   ▶   ▶   ▶   ▶   ▶   ▶   ▶

The goal of this chapter is to provide you with strategies for how to read, analyze, and understand the questions on the *Social Studies: Interpretation of Materials* test and then how to outline and write successful responses.

Introduction to the Question Types

The *Social Studies: Interpretation of Materials* test is intended to assess whether you have the knowledge and skills necessary to be a beginning teacher of teacher of social studies in a secondary school.

The test is composed of five two-part short-answer essay questions that require reading and interpreting social studies materials, drawing inferences from such materials, and relating these materials to knowledge of the individual fields in social studies. Material presented for interpretation can take the form of a map, chart, graph, table, cartoon, diagram, quotation, or an excerpt from a document. The test contains one question from each of the following five fields: United States history, world history, government/civics/ political science, geography, and economics.

What to Study

United States History

Hartz, Bill, Robert Gorn, and Randy W. Roberts. *Constructing the American Past: A Source Book of a People's History,* 2nd ed. Boston: Addison Wesley, 1995.

A widely-used collection of primary sources that also contains extensive commentary on how to use them.

Marius, Richard. *A Short Guide to Writing About History,* 3rd. ed. New York: Longman, 1998.

Chapter 2 deals with issues relating to primary sources.

Raymond M. Hyser and Christopher J. Arndt. *Voices of the American Past: Documents in U.S. History,* 2nd ed. Vol. II. New York: Wadsworth, 2000.

A collection of primary sources with a useful introduction on how to use them.

The National Archives Administration has helpful checklists for what to look for in primary sources: www.archives.gov/digital_classroom/lessons/analysis_worksheets/worksheets.html

The "Do History" Project is a Web site devoted to working with documents concerning "ordinary people" in the past: www.dohistory.org/

World History

The following are three of the better known books of sources in world history. They organize sources chronologically and generally have an introduction and study questions. There may be more recent editions.

Andrea, Alfred, and James Overfield. *The Human Record: Sources of Global History.* Vol. I: *To 1700* and Vol. II: *Since 1500.* Boston: Houghton Mifflin Company, 1990.

Kishlansky, Mark, ed. *Sources of World History: Readings for World Civilization.* Vols. I and II. New York: Harper Collins College Publishers, 1995.

Stearns, Peter, Stephen Gosch, and Erwin Grieshaber. *Documents in World History,* 3rd ed. Vol. I: *The Great Traditions: From Ancient Times to 1500* and Vol. II: *The Modern Centuries: From 1500 to the Present.* New York: Longman, 2003.

The following two volumes of documents are organized by historical questions, and each includes the problem, background, method, questions to consider, and epilogue, as well as the evidence (documents):

Wiesner, Merry; William Bruce Wheeler, Franklin Doeringer, and Kenneth Curtis. *Discovering the Global Past: A Look at the Evidence.* Vol. I: To 1650 and Vol. II: Since 1400. Second Edition (Boston: Houghton Mifflin Company, 2002).

The New York State Regents Web site offers practice tests using review of documents: www.phschool.com/curriculum_support/brief_review/global_history/index.html

Political Science

Almond, Gabriel A., G. Bingham Powell, Jr., Karen Strom, and Russell J. Dalton. *Comparative Politics Today: A World View.* 8th ed. New York: Longman, 2004.

Burns, James MacGregor, J.W. Peltason, Thomas E. Cronin, David B. Magleby, David M. O'Brien, and Paul C. Light . *Government by the People*, 20th ed. New York: Prentice Hall, 2003.

Katznelson, Ira, and Helen V. Milner. *Political Science: State of the Discipline.* New York: W.W. Norton & Company, 2003.

Kegley, Jr., Charles W., and Eugene R. Wittkopf. *World Politics: Trend and Transformation,* 9th ed. New York: Wadsworth, 2004.

University of Michigan. Political Science Resources on the Web: http://www.lib.umich.edu/govdocs/polisci.html

Economics

Baumol, William J., and Alan S. Blinder. *Economics: Principles and Policy*, 9th ed. Mason, OH: Thomson/South-Western, 2002.

Hall, Robert E., and Mark Lieberman. *Economics: Principles and Applications*, 2nd ed. Mason, OH: Thomson/South-Western, 2002.

Mankiw, N. Gregory. *Principles of Economics.* 3rd ed. Mason, Ohio : Thomson/South-Western, 2004.

McConnell, Campbell R., and Stanley L. Brue. *Economics: Principles, Problems, and Policies*, 15th ed. Boston: McGraw-Hill, 2002.

Frank, Robert H., and Ben S. Bernanke. *Principles of Economics*, 2nd ed. Boston: McGraw-Hill, 2004.

Geography

Getis, Arthur, Judith Getis, and Jerome D. Fellmann. *Introduction to Geography*, 9th edition. Boston: McGraw-Hill Higher Education, 2004 .

The best introductory-level overview of physical and human geography. If you can afford only one book, this is the best choice.

Fellmann, Jerome D., Arthur Getis, and Judith Getis. *Human Geography: Landscapes of Human Activities*, 7th edition. New York: McGraw-Hill, 2003.

This is an excellent introductory-level textbook for human and cultural geography. Also includes a section on human actions and environmental impacts. World Population Data included in Appendix B.

McKnight, Tom L. and Darrel Hess. *Physical Geography: A Landscape Appreciation*, 7th ed. Upper Saddle River, NJ: Prentice-Hall, 2003.

Introductory-level textbook for physical geography.

Kuby, Michael, John Harner, and Patricia Gober. *Human Geography in Action*, 3rd ed. New York: John Wiley and Sons, Inc., 2002.

Case studies and hands-on activities.

Rowntree, Les, Martin Lewis, Marie Price, and William Wyckoff. *Diversity Amid Globalization: World Regions, Environment, Development*, 2nd edition. Upper Saddle River, NJ: Prentice Hall, 2003.

Regional approach to geography.

Bergman, Edward F. and William H. Renwick. *Introduction to Geography: People, Places, and Environment*, 2nd ed. Upper Saddle River, NJ: Prentice Hall, 2003.

General geography text.

Hudson, John C., and Edward B. Espenshade, Jr., eds. *Goode's World Atlas*, 20th ed. Skokie: Rand McNally, 2000.

The *School Library Journal* calls it "an impressive amount of information into a relatively small, sturdy package" and "the best deal available in an atlas today." Obtain the latest edition, if possible.

Understanding What the Questions Are Asking

It is impossible to write a successful response to a question unless you thoroughly understand the question. Often test takers jump into their written response without taking enough time to analyze exactly what the question is asking, how many different parts of the question need to be addressed, and how the information in the accompanying quotes, cartoons, charts, or tables needs to be addressed. The time you invest in making sure you understand what the question is asking will very likely pay off in a better performance, as long as you budget your time and do not spend a large proportion of the available time just reading the question.

Examine the overall question closely, then identify what specific questions are being asked, mentally organize your response, and outline your key themes. But leave yourself plenty of time to write your answer. If you think out your response beforehand, your essay will probably be stronger. But ending an essay with the phrase "out of time" will win no extra points from the scorers.

Sample Question 1

To illustrate the importance of understanding the question before you begin writing, let's start with a sample question:

> **"It is, emphatically, the province and duty of the judicial department, to say what the law is....If then, the courts are to regard the Constitution, and the Constitution is superior to an ordinary act of the legislature, the Constitution, and not such ordinary act, must govern the case to which both apply.**
>
> **"Thus...a law repugnant to the Constitution is void."**
>
> **John Marshall, Chief Justice of the United States Supreme Court**
> ***Marbury* v. *Madison*, 1803**

1. **Briefly explain the principle of government stated by the Supreme Court in the excerpt above from the decision in *Marbury* v. *Madison*.**

2. **Based on the excerpt above and your knowledge of United States government, briefly explain one reason why the principle stated in the excerpt might be criticized. Then briefly explain one reason why the principle stated in the excerpt might be supported.**

Identifying the key components of the question

- This question has one quote followed by two questions.

- Read the quote carefully and identify its central concept.

- Read each question carefully and determine how the quote applies to the question.

- Question #1: Briefly explain the principle of government stated by the Supreme Court in the excerpt from *Marbury* v. *Madison*.

- Identify the 1803 *Marbury* v. *Madison* decision as addressing the principle of judicial review, that courts may declare federal and state laws void if they violate the U.S. Constitution. You must understand this principle to write an adequate response.

- Question #2 has two parts; identify each part.

- Briefly explain one reason why judicial review might be criticized.

- Briefly explain one reason why judicial review might be supported.

- If you have relevant historical knowledge, use it.

Organizing your response

Successful responses start with successful planning, either with an outline or with another form of notes. By planning your response, you greatly decrease the chance that you will forget to answer any part of the question. You increase the chance of creating a well-organized response, which is something the scorers look for. Your note-taking space also gives you a place to jot down thoughts whenever you think of them—for example, when you have an idea about one part of the question when you are writing your response to another part. Like taking time to make sure you understand what the question is asking, planning your response is time well invested, although you must keep your eye on the clock so that you leave sufficient time to write your response.

To illustrate a possible strategy for planning a response, let us focus again on the sample question introduced in the previous section. We analyzed the question and found that it asked for a two-part response. You might begin by jotting down those parts on your notes page, leaving space under each. This will ensure that you address each part when you begin writing.

Sample notes—main parts to be answered

Here you start by identifying each part of the question:

I. Explain the principle of government stated by the Supreme Court in *Marbury v. Madison*

II. Based on the quote and your knowledge of U.S. government:

    A. Explain one reason why the principle might be criticized

    B. Explain one reason why the principle might be supported

Sample notes—ideas under each main part

You then might quickly fill out the main ideas you want to address in each part, like this:

I. Explain the principle of government stated by the Supreme Court in *Marbury v. Madison*

    A. Judicial Review

II. Based on the quote and your knowledge of U.S. government:

    A. Explain one reason why the principle might be criticized

        1. Judicial activism

    B. Explain one reason why the principle might be supported

        1. Separation of powers

These are key characteristics that the scorers will look for:

- Answer all parts of the question.
- Give reasons for your answers.
- Demonstrate subject-specific knowledge in your answer.
- Refer to the data in the stimulus.

Sample notes—added ideas

Now look at your notes and add any ideas that would address these characteristics. Notice the additions that are made. This is where you use your knowledge of U.S. government and American constitutional history. What you put here depends on how much you know. The following are some possible responses:

I. Explain the principle of government stated by the Supreme Court in Marbury v. Madison

A. Judicial Review

    1. U.S. Constitution is supreme law of land

    2. Supreme Court asserts authority to declare null and void federal, state laws that contradict Constitution

II. Based on the quote and your knowledge of U.S. government:

A. Explain one reason why the principle might be criticized

    1. Judicial activism

        a. Court may overstep authority, defy will of legislative majorities

        b. Historical examples

            i. Dred Scott v. Sanford—Court asserts Congress may not regulate slavery in federal territories

            ii. Progressive reforms—Court strikes down minimum wage laws, labor laws

            iii. New Deal reforms—Court strikes down A.A.A., N.R.A., threatens to invalidate entire New Deal

B. Explain one reason why the principle might be supported

   1. Separation of powers

      a. Judiciary checks other branches, imposes rule of law

      b. Court imposes constitutional standards of justice on states

      c. Historical examples

         i. *Brown v. Board*—Court desegregates southern schools, applies 14th Amendment equal protection of laws to southern African Americans

         ii. Rights of the Accused—1960s court applies protections guaranteed in Bill of Rights to state as well as federal cases (right to attorney, right against self-incrimination)

You have now created the skeleton of your written response.

Writing your response

Now the important step of writing your response begins. The scorers will not consider your notes when they score your paper, so it is crucial that you integrate all the important ideas from your notes into your actual written response.

Some test takers believe that every written response on a Praxis test has to be in formal essay form—that is, with an introductory paragraph, then paragraphs with the response to the question, then a concluding paragraph. This is the case for very few Praxis tests (e.g., *Writing*). The *Social Studies: Interpretation of Materials* test does **not** require formal essays, so you should use techniques that allow you to communicate information efficiently and clearly. For example, you can use bulleted or numbered lists, or a chart, or a combination of essay and chart.

Returning to our sample question, see below how the outline of the response to the first part of the question can become the final written response. What follows is an actual response by a test taker.

Sample response that received a score of 3 for each part

1. In *Marbury v. Madison*, the Supreme Court, for the first time, declared a law unconstitutional. This was not an enunciated power given to the court in the Constitution, it was implied. The court thereby granted itself the power of judicial review. They declared that it was the court's duty to interpret the laws made by Congress and state legislatures. If a law was found to be inconsistent with the spirit and letter of the Constitution, it

was the court's responsibility to declare the law void. The Constitution, as supreme law of the land, must take precedence over all other laws, and it is the court's duty to see to it.

2. This ruling could be criticized by strict constructionists, those that give a very literal interpretation to the Constitution. They may claim that the court is overstepping its bounds by granting itself powers not explicitly stated in the Constitution. Critics may also claim that this gives the judicial branch unrestrained power over the other two branches of the federal government, destroying the government's delicate balance of power. But proponents of the ruling see the ruling not as a threat to the balance of power, but a part of it. With the power of judicial review, the court places a check on Congress and the executive branch, assuming that the Constitution will not be violated. This interpretation of the ruling has been the dominant one since it was handed down in 1803.

Scoring Commentary

- To earn a score of 3 on Part 1, the essay must briefly explain the concept of judicial review as stated in *Marbury* v. *Madison*. This test taker does so clearly. He or she identifies judicial review by name, then explains that the Constitution is the supreme law of the land, that no federal or state law may violate the Constitution, and that the Supreme Court itself had the authority to interpret laws to determine whether they were consistent with the Constitution. The test taker gives the additional information that *Marbury* marked the first time the Court declared a law unconstitutional and also that judicial review was not a power explicitly given to the judiciary by the Constitution.

- To earn a score of 3 on Part 2, the essay must briefly offer one argument critical of judicial review and one argument in favor of it. This test taker does both. He or she argues that a strict constructionist interpretation of the Constitution may not permit the Supreme Court to invest itself with powers not overtly granted it by the Constitution, and that in so doing the Court may assume an unhealthy degree of political power. The test taker then argues, in support of judicial review, that it secures a balance of power in federal government by placing a check on both the legislative and executive branches. Both arguments are concise and to the point.

Sample response that received a score of 1 for each part

1. The principle stated deals with the concept of material law. That is, law that was created and written down at the time of the constitution and should govern all laws thereafter. It is the job of the judicial department to only make judgements based on what is already written and not to create news while interpreting the constitution.

2. Some probably criticized the ruling as being weak, that is that the Supreme Court should pick out areas where the judges feel strongly about a matter and give guidance to the people. An example might be that the court could have an opinion on whether the United States needed to expand its territory in the Louisiana Purchase or was spending too much on armaments, and because the court was made up of distinguished judges with good backgrounds, they could offer an opinion on it. They could be an activist court in this way.

The excerpt might be supported by people who are believers in the judicial part of the government being the superior part to the executive or legislative branches. These citizens believe that the court, because it is composed of intelligent, educated judges, should have more of a say on what the laws of the country should be. They would prefer this way to depending on Congress, which is subject to politics and whims.

Scoring Commentary

- To write an adequate response to this question, the test taker must understand the concept of judicial review—otherwise all is lost. This essay misinterprets the *Marbury* decision, stating correctly that the Constitution must govern all laws, but also that the judiciary must not make "news" (presumably new laws) while interpreting the Constitution. That is not the point of the decision. Moreover, the writing here is imprecise and a bit confusing.

- Because the writer of this essay does not understand the principle of judicial review in Part 1, it is all but impossible to write an adequate essay criticizing and supporting it in Part 2.

- The arguments offered here are, in any case, puzzling. The test taker argues against Marbury because judges should give guidance to the people, and then uses an unexplained example of the Louisiana purchase and an inappropriate example of arms spending. The test taker argues in favor of Marbury in that some believe the Court should be superior to the other branches of government. This is far from the target.

In conclusison

Whatever approach you take to organizing your response, the important consideration is that your answer be thorough, complete, and detailed. You need to be certain that you do the following:

- Answer all parts of the question.

- Give reasons for your answers.

- Demonstrate subject-specific knowledge in your answer.

- Refer to the data in the stimulus.

Chapter 8
Practice Test—*Social Studies: Interpretation of Materials*

Now that you have worked through strategies and preparation relating to the *Social Studies: Interpretation of Materials* test, you should take the following practice test. This test is an actual Praxis test, now retired. You will probably find it helpful to simulate actual testing conditions, giving yourself 120 minutes to work on the questions. You can use the lined answer pages provided if you wish.

Keep in mind that the test you take at an actual administration will have different questions. You should not expect your level of performance to be exactly the same as when you take the test at an actual administration, since numerous factors affect a person's performance in any given testing situation.

When you have finished the practice questions, you can read through the sample responses with scorer annotations in chapter 9.

THE PRAXIS SERIES

Professional Assessments for Beginning Teachers®

TEST NAME:

Social Studies:

Interpretation of Materials (0083)

Time—60 minutes

5 Questions

Question 1

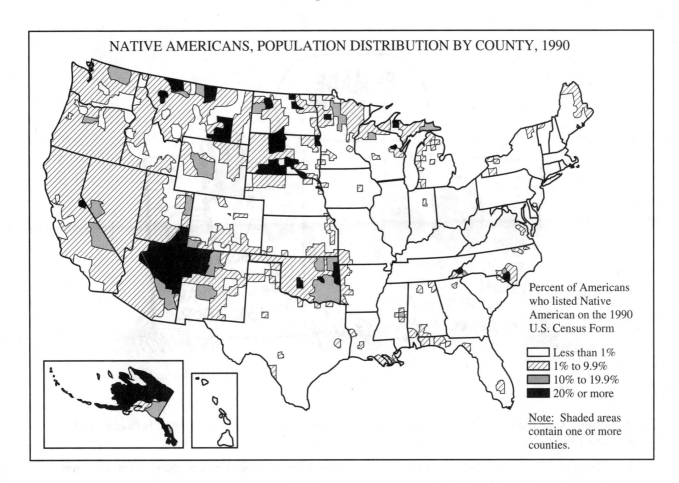

NATIVE AMERICANS, POPULATION DISTRIBUTION BY COUNTY, 1990

Percent of Americans who listed Native American on the 1990 U.S. Census Form

Less than 1%
1% to 9.9%
10% to 19.9%
20% or more

Note: Shaded areas contain one or more counties.

A. Briefly describe the distribution of the Native American population as illustrated in the map above.

B. Discuss TWO specific historical events that were important in creating the population distribution shown above.

NOTES

Question 2

The Philadelphia Inquirer

A. Briefly state the point the cartoonist is making about world affairs in the period between 1945 and 1990.

B. Choose ONE of the countries whose names appear in the cartoon. Explain the political situation that led to the inclusion of this country's name in the cartoon.

NOTES

Question 3

"History shows that many people lose their respect for any religion that relies upon the support of government to spread its faith. The Establishment Clause thus stands as an expression of principle on the part of the Founders of our Constitution that religion is too personal, too sacred, too holy to permit its 'unhallowed perversion' by a civil magistrate."

Engel v. *Vitale, 1962*

A. What is the legal concept expressed in this United States Supreme Court decision?

B Cite an example where this legal concept has affected federal, state, or local government policy, <u>and</u> discuss the important factors involved in the example you have cited, including any conflict or controversy that developed.

NOTES

Question 4

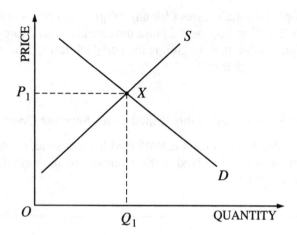

The graph above shows the market for apples.

1. What do points P_1, Q_1, and X represent, respectively?

2. Explain what problem would occur in this market if the market price were to rise above P_1, and explain how the market would eliminate the problem you have identified.

NOTES

Question 5

AGE PATTERNS OF FERTILITY:
UNITED STATES, JAPAN, AND GHANA, 1988

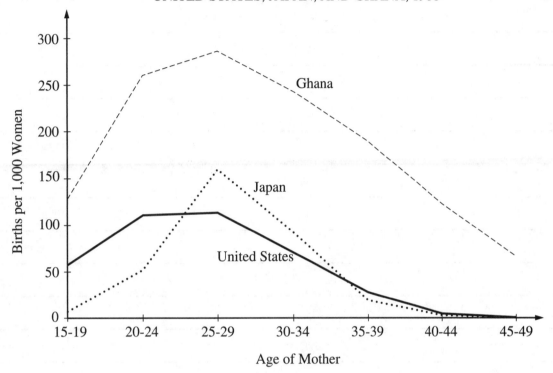

A. Summarize what the graph above indicates about fertility patterns in the United States, Japan, and Ghana in relation to each other.

B. Briefly explain TWO major factors that contribute to the <u>differences</u> in the three fertility patterns shown.

NOTES

Begin your response to Question 1 here.

(Question 1—*Continued*)

Begin your response to Question 2 here.

(Question 2—*Continued*)

Begin your response to Question 3 here.

(Question 3—*Continued*)

Begin your response to Question 4 here.

(Question 4—*Continued*)

Begin your response to Question 5 here.

(Question 5—*Continued*)

Chapter 9
Sample Responses and How They Were Scored—
Social Studies: Interpretation of Materials

▶   ▶   ▶   ▶   ▶   ▶   ▶   ▶   ▶   ▶   ▶   ▶

This chapter presents actual sample responses to the questions in the practice test and explanations for the scores they received.

As discussed in chapter 3, each question on the *Social Studies: Interpretation of Materials* test has two parts and is given two scores, on a scale of 0-3. The General Scoring Guide used to score these parts is reprinted here for your convenience.

Part 1 of the Question

Score	Comment

3 Accurate and complete:

- Shows a clear understanding of the stimulus
- Provides an accurate and complete response

2 Mostly accurate and complete:

- Shows an adequate understanding of the stimulus
- Provides a generally accurate and complete response

1 Inaccurate and incomplete:

- Shows little understanding of the stimulus
- Provides a basically inaccurate and incomplete response

0 Completely inaccurate or inappropriate, blank, off topic, or only a restatement of the prompt

Part 2 of the Question

Score	Comment

3 Accurate and complete:

- Provides the analysis required by the question
- Applies appropriate subject matter knowledge

2 Mostly accurate and complete:

- Provides most of the analysis required by the question
- Applies mostly appropriate subject matter knowledge

1 Inaccurate and incomplete:

- Provides little of the analysis required by the question
- Applies mostly inappropriate subject matter knowledge

0 Completely inaccurate or inappropriate, blank, off topic, or only a restatement of the prompt

Question 1 (U.S. History)

We will now look at four responses to Question 1 and see how the scoring guide was used to rate each response.

Sample response that earned a score of 3 and 2

> The distribution of the Native American population becomes much more dense as one looks westward on the continent. The most densely populated areas are in and around the "four corners," but not as much in Colorado, Montana, the Dakotas, and Oklahoma. There is also a great concentration of Native Americans in Alaska.
>
> One reason why the Native Americans are mostly on the western part of the continent is because as the United States expanded Natives were killed, made to move westward or amalgamated into the dominate culture.
>
> With the Indian Bureau Native Americans were told to move to reservations were they could maintain their cultures and would be helped by the American government. In new Mexico and Arizona, we have Indians who would rather be called Pueblos. They live on land that is not easily cultivated and consequently was of no advantage to the white man.
>
> Native Americans have this population distribution to stay out of the Europeans development of the country. Indians at one time roamed the Plains States, but were relegated to living in the mountains and deserts.

Scoring Commentary

- For an essay to earn a score of 3 on Part 1, the test taker must acknowledge that in the West there is a higher concentration of Native Americans (or lower in the East) and must also make specific reference to the map by noting a region or states by name. The difference between a 2 and a 3 on Part 1 of the *Social Studies: Interpretation of Materials* test is often determined by the degree of specificity with which the essay refers to the map, chart, cartoon, or quote.

- This test taker notes that the Native American population is more dense in the West and mentions several western states by name. The requirements of a 3 score are fulfilled.

- To earn a score of 3 on Part 2, the test taker must describe two historical events that led to the greater concentration of Indians in the West. The essay earns a 2 if only one event is described or two are merely mentioned. The difference between a 2 and a 3 often depends on the degree of development and specificity of the discussion.

- Part 2 of this essay earns a 2, because one historical event is discussed—westward movement onto reservations.

Sample Responses to Question 1, continued

Sample response that earned a score of 2 and 3

A) Native American populations are concentrated in Oklahoma, Arizona, in the Southern U.S. and in Alaska, the Dakotas, in the Northern U.S.

B) The forced march of the Cherokee nation from Tennessee to Oklahoma accounts for the absence of Cherokee in their native lands and the strong concentrations in Oklahoma.

In the 1840-50's the Fitzpatrick treaties first began to use terminology like "concentration" and "reservation" in reference to the relocation of Nat. Am. Groups. The plains Indians were targeted for relocation in the 1860's. Through the Medicine Lodge Treaty and the Fort Laramie Treaty, Cheyenne, Navajo, Sioux, Kiowa, Commanche were relocated to areas outside of overland trade routes. Specifically the Dakotas (Black Hills Area) and area's south of Kansas.

Scoring Commentary

- To earn a score of 2 on Part 1, the writer must show some ability to interpret the map, but may do only one of the two tasks required for a score of 3. This test taker identifies greater concentrations of Native Americans in Oklahoma, Arizona, Alaska, and the Dakotas, but does not make the distinction between the western part of the U.S. as opposed to the eastern part. Consequently, this essay fulfills one of the two requirements for a 3, with no major mistakes, which places it in the 2 range.

- This essay earns a score of 3 on Part 2, because the test taker discusses two historical events responsible for Indian concentrations in the West: the forced march of the Cherokee nation to Oklahoma and the relocation of Plains Indians onto reservations. There is imbalance in the discussion, in that the Cherokee example is less developed than the reservation example (and with a minor error—the Cherokee were forced out of Georgia, not Tennessee). But essays are graded holistically, and there is a great deal of appropriate and specific knowledge in the discussion.

Sample response that earned a score of 1 and 2

1. The native american population is position mostly in the western part of the United States. There are some also in the Midwest, but very little in the eastern part of the U.S.

2. Two historical events that could have contributed to the native American living mostly in the western part of the United States is the "trail of tears," and the Northwest Ordinance. Both of these policies forced the American Indian west. Jackson overturn a supreme court decision and set the moving of Indians west, because he needed the land for white settlers.

> Even through the Indians were accommodating to American ways, they were still forced out of their home and on a trail that killed many of them. The Northwest Ordinance forced Indians west because the land in west was also needed for white settlers. This forced Indians of the reservations given to them by the government to land further west. As America has felt it was their destiny to rule they forgot the American Indian who was here first. Once west, the Indians had no where to go, and so many remained in the western part of the U.S.

Scoring Commentary

- To earn a score of 1 on Part 1, the test taker must demonstrate little or no ability to interpret the map. In this essay, the test taker misreads the map, which identifies the Indian population in each area as a percentage of the total population, not in absolute numbers. (For instance, Native Americans are a larger percentage of the population in South Dakota than in New York, but there are more Indians in New York than in South Dakota). This writer states that most Indians are in the western United States, an assumption the information on the map does not warrant.

- This essay earns a score of 2 on Part 2 because one historical event is discussed correctly. The test taker tells us that Andrew Jackson overturned a Supreme Court decision, forcing American Indians west on the Trail of Tears, along which many died. The discussion of the Northwest Ordinance is not actually correct, in that it did not force Indians out of the territory. (The Ordinance contained a provision stating that Indian lands could not be taken without Indian consent.)

Sample response that earned a score of 1 and 1

> The majority of the Native American population resides in the western half of the United States, including Alaska.
>
> The Native Americans have always had to fight for their territory and were driven west by the "white man." To settle in unoccupied land where they could settle without the threat of total persecution was inviting to the Native Americans. Alaska, Arizona, and New Mexico provided an "open" environment where they could cultivate together an environment of growing and living rather than fighting for land the "white man" wanted.

Scoring Commentary

- This essay earns a score of 1 on Part 1 because the test taker misreads the map. As with the previous test taker, this writer argues that the map shows a majority of Native Americans residing in the western half of the United States. Instead, the map shows that Indians are a larger percentage of the total population in the western half of the U.S.

- To earn a score of 1 on Part 2, the essay must provide little or no specific historical information, and this test taker does no better than that level of achievement. This essay tells us that Native Americans were driven west by the "white man," but with no historical references—no events, people, or legislation. This essay is too uninformed to be an adequate response.

Question 2 (World History)

We will look at four responses to Question 2 and see how the scoring guide was used to rate each response.

Sample response that earned a score of 3 and 3

1. USA and the USSR, locked in an ideological conflict in the decades following WWII, attempted to maximize their influences by interfering in the political and national affairs in the countries listed. This was ostensibly to protect those nation's interests from the supposedly "evil" intentions of the opposite superpower, hence the adolescent "He made me do it" logic lampooned in the cartoon.

2. Vietnam – In the years following WWII, this French colonial possession underwent a nationalistic revolt led by Ho Chi Minh that ultimately led to the partitioning of the country into Communist northern and U.S.-supported southern sections after the French defeat at Dien Bien Phu in 1954. The North, never accepting the status quo, began a nearly twenty-year quest to unite the country under Communist rule (forcibly, if need be). Recognizing this, the U.S. began to intefere by supporting a series of corrupt, oppressive, but pro-Western governments in the South, ultimately becoming fully involved militarily. This contributed immeasurably to the conflict which ravaged the land and population of Vietnam.

Scoring Commentary

- To earn a score of 3 on Part 1, the test taker must correctly interpret the cartoon by doing three things: demonstrate that both the United States and the former Soviet Union were involved in the internal affairs of the countries listed; identify this as an outgrowth of the Cold War; and acknowledge that each superpower blamed the other for their actions or that each was equally guilty.

- In this essay all three requirements are fulfilled for a score of 3 on Part 1. The writer identifies the U.S. and the former Soviet Union as involved in ideological conflict after the Second World War (the test taker may identify the Cold War by name but is not required to use those actual words); notes that each attempted to maximize its influence by interfering in the political and national affairs of the countries listed; and that each did so for the ostensible purpose of protecting those countries from the evil influence of the opposing superpower.

- To earn a score of 3 on Part 2, the test taker must provide an accurate account of the political situation in one of the countries listed and also indicate the means by which the U.S. or the former Soviet Union became involved.

- This test taker provides a nice, concise account of Vietnam after the Second World War and the beginnings of America's subsequent involvement. All of the information is correct and relevant, and there is enough detail to place the essay in the top category.

Sample response that earned a score of 2 and 3

In the cartoon, the cartoonist is making the point that each of the superpowers, the Soviet Union, and the United States have committed crimes in various countries because of the competition between them. However both are seen as equally guilty as both are in pillories as punishment.

Guatemala is a case in point of a U.S. crime. In 1954, the election of a new president in Guatemala, President Arbenz caused alarm within the government of the United States. Advocating as he did land reformation, Arbenz threatened the interests of the countries biggest landowner, the United Fruit Company. What outraged them the most however was that Arbenz proposed paying compensation based on the company's property tax payments to Guatemala. Needless to say this was far below actual value.

The Dulles brothers, one Secretary of State, the other director of the CIA, both having close ties to United Fruit, convinced President Eisenhower that Arbenz was part of a world-wide communist conspiracy and that he wanted to nationalize private property like a communist. In a CIA operation called "Operation Success", Arbenz was overthrown and assassinated by a CIA army operating out of a neighboring countries. His CIA appointed successors instituted a long period of clandestine disappearances and assassinations of political opponents bucked by a openly military dictatorship.

Scoring Commentary

- This essay earns a score of 2 on Part 1, because the test taker does two of the three things asked. The writer notes that both the United States and the former Soviet Union have committed crimes in other countries (the wording here is a little vague, but it is sufficient) and states that both superpowers are equally guilty. Involvement in other nations as an outgrowth of the Cold War is not identified. The test taker does acknowledge that there was competition between the two superpowers, but the nature of that competition is not identified.

- This essay earns a score of 3 on Part 2, because the writer provides an accurate and factual account of the political situation in Guatemala and indicates the means by which the U.S. became involved. It is an excellent and brief essay that provides more information than is required for a 3.

Sample Responses to Question 2, continued

Sample response that earned a score of 2 and 1

> The cartoons illustrate the occurrence of the cold war rivalries in small countries affairs. Ultimately, Russia and the U.S. are shackled to their political involvements in world affairs and subject to the influence of or demands of smaller nations.
>
> The most obvious choice for the cartoon's discussion is Cuba. Cuba is supported by the Soviet Union and has been due to the cold war sediment of the appearing figure (bear, Sam). The U.S. under the framework of the Monroe Doctrine must control the political atmosphere of the region in which Cuba is part. Thus situations like the Bay of Pigs will continue as long as these world powers allow themselves to be tied to the involvement of smaller countries.

Scoring Commentary

- This essay earns a score of 2 on Part 1, because two of the three requirements are satisfied. The writer identifies Cold War rivalries between the United States and the former Soviet Union and notes that both were involved in the affairs of other nations—shackled to political involvements and the demands of smaller nations. This test taker does not address the issue of each superpower's blaming the other for its actions or of each superpower's being equally guilty.

- For an essay to earn a score of 2 on Part 2, the test taker must provide a general explanation of the political situation in one of the countries listed. This writer does not do that. He or she informs us that Cuba was supported by the former Soviet Union, but the explanation goes no further. The Bay of Pigs is mentioned, but what that was and why it was significant are not identified. Had the test taker explained the invasion at Cuba's Bay of Pigs as America's involving itself in Cuba's domestic affairs or introduced some specific information, Part 2 would have earned a score of 2.

Sample response that earned a score of 1 and 1

> The cartoonist is trying to indicate errors made in world affairs and no one taking responsibility for the decisions made. In a way the cartoonist could be saying that in all these political situations there was no way out and thus a price had to be paid.
>
> The representation of a U.S. president and the inclusion of Vietnam are clear indications of erroneous world affairs. The Vietnam created more havoc and chaos than it created a sincerity of democratic beliefs.

Scoring Commentary

- This essay earns a score of 1 on Part 1, because the writer demonstrates little understanding of the cartoon. The Cold War It is not identified, the United States and the former Soviet Union are not identified as superpowers, and there is no acknowledgement of either superpower's interference in the domestic affairs of other countries. The essay satisfies none of the requirements.

- This essay earns a score of 1 on Part 2 because, in the example of Vietnam, the test taker demonstrates no understanding of the political situation in Vietnam and does not acknowledge that the United States became involved in that country. The response satisfies none of the requirements for an adequate essay.

Question 3 (Political Science)

We will now look at four responses to Question 3 and see how the scoring guide was used to rate each response.

Sample response that earned a score of 3 and 3

The Engel v. Vitale decision supports the separation of church and state. This is the principle that the United States was founded as when the first immigrants arrived from Europe. In today's society a prime example of this issue is prayer in public schools. More conservative republican governments have expressed the desire to have prayer re-established in the school system. Today legally, this can only be found in private schools. The general populace would not accept prayer in public schools for that would be enforcing a certain religion and one of of our first rights granted to us in the Bill of Rights is the freedom of religion. From time to time the legislature tries to drum up support for a bill to allow this breach of the separation of church and state, yet it is generally not taken seriously and not accepted by the citizens of the U.S.

Scoring Commentary

- To earn a score of 3 on Part 1, the essay needs to satisfy two requirements: it must correctly identify the concept expressed in the 1962 Supreme Court decision *Engel* v. *Vitale* as separation of church and state, and it must also identify the concept as based on the Bill of Rights or the First Amendment. (It may use the term Establishment Clause, but is not required to do so.)

- In this essay, the test taker does both. The writer notes that *Engel* supports the separation of church and state and later tells us that freedom of religion is granted in the Bill of Rights.

- To earn a score of 3 on Part 2, the essay must satisfy two requirements. It must provide an accurate account of any specific issue for which separation of church and state has affected government policy (the topic of this discussion is virtually always prayer in public schools), and it must also present the views or arguments of each side.

Sample Responses to Question 3, continued

- The writer of this essay does both. The issue here is prayer in public schools. In discussing advocacy of school prayer, this test taker states that "conservative republican governments" periodically attempt to reestablish prayer in the public school system, something legal only in private schools. In regard to the opposing view, this test taker argues that school prayer is unacceptable to a majority of the population because it means the state would enforce a particular religion, which is a violation of the First Amendment.

- The account of the argument of prayer opponents is accurate and to the point. Although the account of the argument of prayer advocates is not as strong, this test taker does address both sides of the issue.

Sample response that earned a score of 2 and 2

The legal concept of the quote is a seperation between the powers of church and state. Neither religion nor public government should be allowed to enforce, regulate, or otherwise control one another. Both should be treated as seperate and individualized entities.

The most prominent example of recent political events is that of prayer in schools. The Court has ruled that prayer in school is disallowed, because schools are a function of government regulation. Religion thus has no place in a public school setting. Recent efforts have been made to allow some functions of private worship within schools. The requirement for such a proposal is that private worship allows students to practice their religion without pedigogic influence. Opponents of this view say there is no room for religion of any kind in a public school format. In essence, any allowance of religion is an endorsement.

Scoring Commentary

- To earn a score of 2 on Part 1, the essay must correctly identify separation of church and state, either by name or by inference. Unlike an essay that earns a score of 3, it does not acknowledge the foundations of separation of church and state in the Bill of Rights or the First Amendment.

- The writer of this essay identifies church/state separation by name and then defines it but makes no mention of the Bill of Rights.

- To earn a score of 2 on Part 2, the essay should provide a more generalized description than one would find in an essay that scores 3, but also provide some discussion of the arguments involved in the controversy.

- This test taker addresses the opponents-of-school-prayer side by stating that schools are subject to government regulation and that religion consequently has no place in them. The advocates-of-school-prayer argument given in this essay makes no sense. The test taker states that those who want to permit private worship in schools do so in order to allow students to practice their religion without pedagogic influence.

- Generally, the language is less precise and its meanings less clear than in the previous essay.

Sample response that earned a score of 2 and 1

The legal concept expressed is that of separation of the church and state.

A federal example of this concept being addressed would be the taking of religion from public schools. It shouldn't be the state supporting any religion if it can't support all of them equally in front of the students. Especially if we are teaching them how to work in this current world. Conflict developed because certain groups didn't want a balanced view of religion and wanted their view expressed to their children.

Scoring Commentary

- This essay earns a score of 2 on Part 1, because the test taker correctly identifies the concept of separation of church and state (which lifts it above a score of 1) but does not identify the base of church-state separation in the Bill of Rights or the First Amendment (which keeps the essay from earning a score of 3).

- This essay earns a score of 1 on Part 2 because, as the question-specific scoring guide says, it "offers vague generalities and opinions only." The test taker states the removal of religion (not prayer) from public schools as an example, which is incorrect. The test taker then offers his or her own opinion (not that of the groups involved) that the state should not support any religion if it does not support them all equally. The essay finishes with the statement that certain groups did not want a balanced view of religion, a mostly confusing statement.

Sample response that earned a score of 1 and 1

The legal concept expressed in the United States Supreme Court decision in Engel V. Vitale, 1962 is that any group, religious or social, etc. has the right to congregate and espouse its views and practices as long as no federal or state laws ar broken or any individual's rights are violated.

There are hundreds of groups that meet and organize in the U.S. that are protected by the constitution and Supreme Court that millions of people find less than desirable, for instance the Klu Klux Klan. The beliefs and practice of the Klan have prompted much political and civil unrest and have created much controversey, however their right to meet is protected. Of course their acts of violence must be held in check by state and federal laws and law enforcement, but their promotion of racism and intolerance cannot be persecuted without violating the very standards and rights they wish to take from minorities. The Establishment Clause is quite the double edged sword in some instances.

Sample Responses to Question 3, continued

Scoring Commentary

- This essay earns a score of 1 on Part 1 because the test taker misidentifies the concept expressed in *Engel* v. *Vitale*. The writer identifies it as the right to congregate and espouse views rather than separation of church and state. The test taker uses the term Establishment Clause but uses it incorrectly. There is no mention of religion in this essay.

- This essay earns a score of 1 on Part 1 because its discussion is irrelevant and inappropriate to the concept of separation of church and state. The example of the Ku Klux Klan is a good one for a discussion of free speech issues, but the question did not ask about that.

Question 4 (Economics)

We will now look at four responses to Question 4 and see how the scoring guide was used to rate each response.

Sample response that earned a score of 3 and 3

X represents equilibrium price and quantity. This is the price and quantity which buyers and sellers are willing and able to supply and (consequently consumers buy) all the apples produced. This price and quantity also is referred to a the "ideal" price/quantity because all supplied at this price level will be bought. (there is no shortage or surplus). "Equilibrium" means that supply and demand are in perfect balance.

If the market price rose above P1 for apples, then as apples became more expensive and the price rises—producers would seek to produce more apples at the higher price. Unfortunately, for the producers—the price increase will probably be short-lived—because people will probably buy fewer apples at the higher price. People generally (demand) buy fewer at the higher prices begin to look for good substitutes (other fruits). As people demand fewer apples— the producers eventually will drop the price (in an effort to sell their surplus at a cheaper price—remember apples are perishable). As the demand decreases—the equilibrium price/quantity (X) are forced back down. This interaction of supply/demand (this is <u>only theoretical—no</u> other complicating factors) explains the self-correcting principle of the market— first explained by Adam Smith (Wealth of Nations—1776) in his tenets or capitalism.

Scoring Commentary

- To earn a score of 3 on Part 1, the essay needs to do three things: identify P_1 as equilibrium price; identify Q_1 as equilibrium quantity; and identify X as the equilibrium point at which quantity supplied equals quantity demanded.

- This essay does all three things. Although the test taker does not specifically refer to P_1 and Q_1 in explaining Part 1, he or she does identify equilibrium price and equilibrium quantity and indicate that equilibrium point is the point at which supply and demand are in perfect balance.

- To earn a score of 3 on Part 2, the test taker needs to explain that when the market price rises above P_1, then quantity supplied will exceed quantity demanded, or create a surplus; and it must explain how the market would eliminate the problem—that the increased price will discourage consumers from buying, which will decrease the demand and thus create a decrease in price.

- This essay does all of those things. The test taker argues that if the market price rises above P_1 for apples, then consumers will buy fewer apples at the higher price, perhaps buying alternative fruits. A decline in demand will force prices back down to equilibrium point.

Sample response that earned a score of 2 and 2

1. Point P_1 on the graph represents the ideal price to be set for apples. Point Q_1 is the quantity of apple to be produced. Point X, is where the price and quantity of apples meets to satisfy the respective supply and demand curves for this item.

2. If the market price for apples were to rise above P_1 the demand would decrease. Consumers don't want to pay high prices for an item that has so many equally valuable alternatives (other fruit). To eliminate that problem the quantity would have to be decreased to allow demand to recover. Slowly increase quantity and lower the price in order to restore the equilibrium between supply and demand.

Scoring Commentary

- To earn a score of 2 on Part 1, the essay must correctly identify two of the three points on the chart. The writer of this essay correctly identifies point X as the point at which price and quantity meet to satisfy both supply and demand, and the test taker identifies P_1 as the ideal price. But the test taker identifies Q_1 somewhat confusingly as the quantity of apples to be produced.

- To earn a score of 2 on Part 2, the test taker must either explain both parts of the question—but with some inaccuracies—or discuss only one part of the question. Both parts of the question are discussed in this essay, but with some inaccuracies. The test taker correctly argues that if the market price rose above P_1, demand would decrease. He or she correctly argues that in response, the quantity/supply must be reduced to allow demand to recover. Then the test taker reverses that argument by stating that increasing the quantity and lowering the price would restore equilibrium.

Sample Responses to Question 4, continued

Sample response that earned a score of 1 and 3

> IN THE GRAPH OF SUPPLY VERSUS DEMAND, POINTS P_1, Q_1, AND X REPRESENT THE MAXIMUM PRICE, THE MAXIMUM QUANTITY, AND THEIR IDEAL CONVERGENCE AS THE MARKET WILL BEAR THEM.
>
> WERE THE PRICE TO RISE ABOVE P_1, DEMAND WOULD DECREASE, RESULTING IN A SURPLUS QUANTITY. NATURALLY, PRODUCTION WOULD INITIALLY TEND TO DECREASE IN RESPONSE TO THE SURPLUS, SO LONG AS THAT SURPLUS WAS PROJECTED TO EXIST. IN THE PRESENCE OF SURPLUS, HOWEVER, THE NEW PRICE WOULD NOT LIKELY LONG PERSIST. INSTEAD, THE PRICE WOULD NATURALLY RETURN TO P1 AS DEMAND DID NOT MEET SUPPLY EXPECTATIONS.

Scoring Commentary

- This essay earns a score of 1 for Part 1 because the writer seems to understand Point X, but it incorrectly identifies P_1 as maximum price and incorrectly identifies Q_1 as maximum quantity.

- This essay earns a score of 3 for Part 2 because the explanation—that if the price rose above P_1, demand would decrease, there would be a surplus, and the market would correct itself because production would decrease until the price returned to P_1—is consistent with the question-specific scoring guide.

Sample response that earned a score of 1 and 1

> 1. The Points P_1, Q_1 and X represents the point of equilibrium where production (supply) meets Demand.
>
> If the market price rose above the P_1 there would a resulting decrease in the demand and an increase in supply. Therefore, with a surplus of production, the law of equilibrium would bring the demand in compliance with production by reducing the prices, and thus stimulating the demand again.

Scoring Commentary

- To earn a score of 1 on Part 1, the test taker must correctly identify no more than one of the three points on the chart. The writer of this essay identifies X as the equilibrium point at which supply and demand meet. But the test taker incorrectly identifies P_1 and Q_1 as being identical to point X.

- To earn a score of 1 on Part 2, the test taker must discuss only one part of the question and/or be largely inaccurate. In this brief essay, the test taker argues that if the market price rose above P_1, there would be a decrease in demand (which is correct). She or he further argues that the law of equilibrium would bring demand in compliance with production by reducing the prices, which is a misstatement. Rather, the law of equilibrium would bring production in compliance with demand.

Question 5 (Geography)

We will now look at four responses to Question 5 and see how the scoring guide was used to rate each response.

Sample response that earned a score of 3 and 3

In the United States fertility patterns increase slowly from ages 15 to 24 at which point they level off until age 29 and start decreasing slowly until they become almost non-existent at age 49.

In Japan, fertility rates climb from near zero at age 19 to a sharp increase and high point at age 29. There is a sharp decline at age 30 and rates become non-existent at age 49.

In Ghana, fertility rates start off relatively high at age 15 and rise steadily until age 20 where rates plateau. At age 29, rates start to decrease rapidly but still stay relatively high at age 49.

The striking difference in these rates is the number of births to women under the age of 20. In Japan this is pretty non-existent, the United States has a slightly higher rate at about 50 per 1000 births, but Ghana increases about three times that of the United States at approximately 150 per 1000 births. The reason for this is because of differences in society. In Japan, society is much more strict as there is a focus on education and occupational training for the young men and women. In the united States, social restrictions are much more lax for teens which gives way to a rise in teenage pregnancy rates. In Ghana, society is much less developed or dependent upon education and training for the young, therefore many young women are married and having families at a much younger age.

Because the United States has many more opportunities for women outside the home, many women postpone having children until they have established their careers. This is why the United States has a much lower fertility rate for women aged 20 through 35 and a higher rate for women aged 35 through 45 than Japan where women in the workforce is less common.

In Ghana, since it is not as developed as the United States or Japan, effective forms of birth control are not available, therefore Ghana's fertility rates remain higher than those of the U.S. and Japan from ages 15 through 50.

Sample Responses to Question 5, continued

Scoring Commentary

- Since each part of this question has multiple elements, each part must address all of these elements to earn a score of 3.

- To earn a score of 3 on Part 1, the test taker must address both age patterns and number of births in each of three countries: the United States, Japan, and Ghana.

- The writer of this essay does all of these things. In the first three sentences, the test taker refers specifically to the ages at which birth rates rise and decline in each of the three countries. In the three sentences that follow, the test taker contrasts—using numbers from the graph—the differences in birth rates between the three countries.

- To earn a score of 3 on Part 2, the test taker must clearly discuss two factors that explain the differences in the three fertility patterns. The writer of this essay does more than is needed for the three. The test taker argues that teen birth rates are low in Japan because of the emphasis on education and occupational training. In the U.S., by contrast, there are fewer restrictions on teenagers and thus higher rates of teen pregnancies. Ghana, on the other hand, is a "less developed" nation, there are fewer opportunities for education, and people have families at a younger age.

- The test taker continues by arguing that because there are more job opportunities for women in the U.S., many postpone childbirth until they have established their careers, and consequently there are higher birth rates at later ages. And finally, the comparative lack of birth control devices in Ghana explains higher birth rates there than in the U.S. or Japan.

Sample response that earned a score of 1 and 2

Fertility patterns in the three countries Ghana, Japan, and the United States follow the same trend in that births increase from the ages from 15–29, and decrease from ages 29–49. Women in Ghana have far more birth than do women in Japan or the U.S.

Two major factors that influences these birth rates are the level of industrialization in the country and the size or land area of the country. Both Japan and the U.S. are highly industrialized nations and in this setting children have a net cost to the family. In Ghana children do not cost, but can add the families income. In Ghana food is grown by the family, so the more help (children) the family gets, the more food the family has. In Japan and the US. food production is not done by the individual family, so it is not an advantage to have many children. The size of the country and amount of livable land plays a roll in how many children are concieved. For example the population density in Japan in very high, they need more land, so the birth rate is forced down. Ghana and the U.S. have more room to populate.

Scoring Commentary

- This essay gets a score of 1 on Part 1, because one of the two major discrepancies is omitted. In the first two sentences, the test taker refers to all three countries and to the age of fertility in these countries, but not to absolute number of births.

- This essay gets a score of 2 on Part 2, because only one correct factor is discussed. The test taker discusses all three nations and argues that Japan and the United States are industrialized nations where large families entail high costs. In an agricultural nation like Ghana, on the other hand, children are economic assets and consequently large families are economically desirable. This is a good argument, but to earn a score of 3, an essay needs two arguments.

- The second argument in this essay is wrong and therefore does not receive any credit. The test taker argues that geographical size in these three countries determines the birth rate. Japan is densely populated, which forces low birth rates, whereas Ghana and the U.S. have more space for population growth. This contradicts the information on the graph that the birth rates of the U.S. and Japan are roughly equal and ignores the fact that Ghana is relatively densely populated.

Sample response that earned a score of 2 and 1

1. I am asked to summarize what the given graph indicates about fertility patterns in the U.S., Japan, and Ghana. The graph indicates that more young girls in Ghana give birth than in Japan, or the U.S. It also shows that there are more births at any age in Ghana than the U.S. or Japan. It shows that the 25–29 age group in Japan are more likely to give birth than other age groups.

2. Two factors that contribute to the differences in the fertility patterns in the graph are that Japan requires its citizens to restrict themselves to one child per couple and that the U.S. has more women in the workforce and they put off having children until they are older. Even though Japanese couples do at times have more than one child, their government rewards those who do only have one child. This is their way of controlling the population in their country.

Scoring Commentary

- This essay earns a score of 2 on Part 1, because the writer comments accurately on all three countries and discusses age of fertility but does not specifically discuss absolute number of births. The test taker notes that more women give birth at a young age in Ghana than in the United States and Japan, and that Ghana has a higher birth rate at all ages. The specific reference is made in the essay to the 25–29 age-group in Japan, which is mostly correct, but the test taker needs also to use the numbers on the "Births per 1,000 Women" side of the graph.

Sample Responses to Question 5, continued

- This essay receives a score of 1 for Part 2 because it is wrong. The test taker argues that Japan restricts its citizens to one child per couple. The writer confuses Japan with China, a mistake that is large enough to overwhelm the accurate information in the essay (that American women postpone childbirth because they are active in the workforce).

Sample response that earned a score of 1 and 1

> The graph seem to indicate a consistent rise in births after the age of twenty with a general cap at the age of twenty nine or thirty.
> With respect to poplutions, the introduction of education and birth control methods to the U.S. and Japan reflect a more stable birth rate in relation to the socio-economic conditions in Ghana.

Scoring Commentary

- This essay earns a score of 1 for Part 1 because it has very little information, and much of the information is inaccurate. The test taker argues that there is a consistent rise in births after age 20. Actually, the chart shows a steady rise in births after age 15, and in Japan the birth rate stabilizes after age 20. The test taker also argues that there is a general cap in the birth rate by age 30. The chart shows birth rates in each country declining by age 25.

- This essay earns a score of 1 for Part 2 because its explanation for contrasting birth patterns makes no sense. The test taker argues that education and birth control reflect a more stable birth rate in the United States and Japan. The language obscures rather than clarifies the point here. The test taker should explain factors that *contribute* to rather than *reflect* the fertility patterns.

Chapter 10
Preparing for the *Social Studies: Pedagogy* Test

► ► ► ► ► ► ► ► ► ► ► ►

The goal of this chapter is to provide you with strategies for how to read, analyze, and understand the questions on the *Social Studies: Pedagogy* test and then how to write successful responses.

Introduction to the Question Types

The *Social Studies: Pedagogy* test is designed to assess how well a prospective teacher of secondary social studies can design a unit plan and a lesson plan, and provide explanations for the appropriateness of the activities selected.

The test is composed of two case studies, each with five questions.

The first case study is formulated to evaluate your knowledge of either United States or world history and your ability to design an appropriate unit for a secondary-level course. A choice of two unit topics is provided. You are given five tasks (which the test refers to as "questions," although they are not posed as questions):

1. To select a central subject matter topic for the unit and explain why the topic is important

2. To select two additional important topics, which must be distinct from each other and from the central topic

3. To identify a key social studies concept that is essential to one of the three topics you have selected and explain in what way it is essential

4. To describe a metaphor, analogy, or historical parallel that you might use to help a student understand the concept you identified in task 3

5. To develop two questions for class discussion that would help students understand either the subject matter topics or the concept; these questions must require students to use cognitive abilities above the level of factual recall, and at least one of the questions must have an explicit interdisciplinary connection

The second case study is formulated to evaluate your knowledge of government/civics/political science, economics, or geography, and your ability to design an appropriate lesson plan for a unit in a secondary-level course. A choice of three courses and units is provided. You are given five tasks (also referred to on the test as "questions"):

1. To identify a topic for the focus of the lesson and explain why this topic warrants a full class period within the unit

2. To write an objective for the lesson topic identified in task 1; this objective must be measurable or observable

3. To identify a teaching strategy for this objective and explain why this teaching strategy is appropriate for the objective

4. To write an essay examination question to measure students' level of achievement for the objective identified in task 2; this examination question must require students to use cognitive abilities above the level of factual recall

5. To describe an alternative method you could use to evaluate students' level of achievement of the objective identified in task 2; you are also to explain why this method is appropriate for the objective

What to Study

Success on this test is not simply a matter of learning more about how to respond to constructed-response questions. Success on the test requires real knowledge of the field. As mentioned above, the test evaluates your knowledge of United States (or world) history, plus government/civics/political science, economics, or geography, as well as your familiarity with strategies for teaching social studies.

It therefore would serve you well to read books and review notes on social studies pedagogy, and to familiarize yourself with the subject matter content in United States or world history and in government/civics/political science, economics, or geography. Because the test is intended to assess the preparation of a prospective teacher of secondary school social studies, the subject matter content of the test is chosen from topics usually included in such courses. One good way, therefore, to prepare for the subject matter dimension of the test would be to begin by examining the tables of contents of several typical secondary school textbooks and seeing what unit topics are generally included and how these topics are organized. For example, most secondary school United States history courses will include units on westward expansion. Familiarity with the historical content of the topics most often included will help give focus to your review of subject matter content.

The social studies pedagogy dimension of the test is carefully interwoven with the subject matter content. You are asked for specific teaching strategies only in Case Study II, the lesson plan. Both case studies, however, ask you to formulate methods of evaluation and to design questions that require more than factual recall. Therefore, to become adept at linking content and pedagogy for the test, you should review the types of questions (i.e., analysis, application, evaluation, and synthesis) and practice writing such questions for a variety of topics usually included in a secondary social studies course.

Understanding What the Questions Are Asking

It is impossible to write a successful response to a question unless you thoroughly understand the question. Often test takers jump into their written response without taking enough time to analyze exactly what the question is asking, how many different parts of the question need to be addressed, and how the five questions for each case study are interrelated. The time you invest in making sure you understand what the question is asking will very likely pay off in a better performance, as long as you budget your time and do not spend too much of the available time just reading the question.

Sample Question: Case Study I

To illustrate the importance of understanding the question before you begin writing, let's start with a sample question:

Option A	**Option B**
Course: United States History	**Course: World History**
Unit: The Cold War	**Unit: Imperialism and Colonialism**

First you must choose between Option A (the United States History unit) and Option B (the World History unit). You *must* write about one of the two options offered. A response, no matter how brilliant, based on a unit topic *not* offered on the test will receive a score of 0, because it will be considered "off topic."

Once you have selected the option you want to work on, you then proceed to answer the five interrelated questions.

- **Question 1** asks you to pick a topic you consider *central* to the unit—that is, a topic that *must be studied* if the unit is to be understood. In your explanation for your selection of this topic, tell why this topic is central. Remember that you are being graded on your knowledge of content as well as pedagogy, so be sure your remarks refer to the specifics of the historical time period.

- **In Question 2,** you must identify two additional subject matter topics that you think are critical for teaching the unit. To receive full credit for your response to this question, your topics must be important *and* they must be clearly distinct from each other *and* from the topic you selected for Question 1. For example, if your subject matter topic for Question 1 was "African Colonies of European Nations," "Cecil Rhodes and British South Africa" as a topic for Question 2 would *not* be considered "clearly distinct." "Economic Causes and Effects of Imperialism" and "British Imperialism in India" would be considered "clearly distinct" both from "African Colonies of European Nations," your topic in Question 1, and from each other.

- **In Question 3,** you must identify a key social studies concept that is essential to one or more of the three topics you have identified in Questions 1 and 2. To receive full credit, your answer must be expressed as a concept (an idea applied to various subjects and time periods), *not* as an additional topic. For example, "protectionism" might be a possible concept to use in Question 3. Your explanation, to receive full credit, must show how the concept relates to one of the three topics. Here you would explain how the imposition of tariffs to create captive markets was related to the topic of "Economic Causes and Effects of Imperialism."

  Again, remember that you are being evaluated partly on subject matter content, not just on social studies pedagogy.

- **Question 4** asks you to describe a metaphor, analogy, or historical parallel you might use to help students understand the concept (in this example "protectionism"). To receive full credit, your metaphor, analogy, or historical parallel *must* relate to "protectionism." If your response relates instead to one of the three topics mentioned in Questions 1 and 2, it will not receive full credit. Again, in your explanation of why this is an appropriate metaphor, analogy, or historical parallel, your response must reveal your knowledge of pedagogy and of subject matter content.

- **Question 5** asks you to develop *two* questions for class discussion that would help students understand either the concept or one of the three topics you have chosen. Notice that there are four components to a complete response:

  1. There are two questions.

  2. The two questions relate to either the concept or the three topics you have chosen in Questions 1 and 2 .

  3. Your questions *require students to use cognitive abilities above the factual-recall level.*

  4. One of the questions must make an explicit connection between history and one or more social science disciplines. Be sure you *identify* the discipline. Do not expect the scorer to figure out the discipline to which you are alluding.

Organizing your response

Successful responses start with successful planning, either with an outline or with another form of notes. By planning your response, you greatly decrease the chance that you will forget to answer any of the questions related to the case study. You increase the chance of creating a well-organized response, which is something the scorers look for. Your note-taking space also gives you a place to jot down thoughts whenever you think of them—for example, when you have an idea about one of the questions while you are writing your response to another question. Like taking time to make sure you understand what each question is asking, planning your response is time well invested, although you must keep track of the time so that you leave sufficient time to write your response.

To illustrate a possible strategy for planning a response, let us focus again on the sample case study introduced in the previous section. We analyzed the case and looked at all five of the related questions. You might begin by jotting down a brief heading for each question on your notes page, leaving space under each. This will ensure that you address each question when you begin writing.

Sample notes—main parts to be answered

Here you start by identifying each question related to the topic:

> (1) Subject Matter Topic 1
>
> (2) Subject Matter Topic 2
>
> Subject Matter Topic 3
>
> (3) Social Studies Concept
>
> (4) Metaphor/Analogy/Historical Parallel
>
> (5) Questions for Class Discussion

You then might quickly fill out the main ideas you want to address in each part, like this (in this example, we have chosen Option B):

Sample notes—ideas under each main part

> (1) Subject Matter Topic 1—Scramble for Africa
>
> (2) Subject Matter Topic 2—How the imperial powers were able to rule their colonies
>
> Subject Matter Topic 3—Forms of colonial resistance
>
> (3) Social Studies Concept—Social Darwinism (used as justification)
>
> (4) Metaphor/Analogy/Historical Parallel—life as a footrace

(5) Questions for Class Discussion

    1. economic factors

    2. effects on geography

You have now created the skeleton of your written response.

Writing your response

Now the important step of writing your response begins. The scorers will not consider your notes when they score your paper, so it is crucial that you integrate all the important ideas from your notes into your actual written response.

To earn the highest number of points from the scorers you will need to do all of the following:

- Answer all five related questions.

- Demonstrate clear understanding of relevant subject matter and pedagogy.

- Provide appropriate, accurate, and complete explanations or supporting information.

Some test takers believe that every written response on a Praxis test has to be in formal essay form—that is, with an introductory paragraph, then paragraphs with the response to the question, then a concluding paragraph. This is the case for very few Praxis tests (e.g., *English* and *Writing*). The *Social Studies: Pedagogy* test does **not** require formal essays, and in fact for many of the questions a simple title (e.g., of a lesson) or a single paragraph of explanation is all that is required.

Returning to our sample case study, see below how the outline of the responses to the related question can be developed to become the final written response. (Note that Question 2 needs no further elaboration.) What follows is an actual response by a test taker.

Sample response that received a score of 3

(1) Subject Matter Topic 1—The Scramble for Africa

The Scramble for Africa represents western imperialism during its most intense phase, at the end of the nineteenth century. Students should know how industrialized European powers were able to divide up almost an entire continent among themselves in twenty years or so, because this has had major political, economic and social consequences down to the present day.

(2) Subject Matter Topic 2—How the imperial powers were able to rule their colonies

Subject Matter Topic 3—Forms of colonial resistance

(3) Social Studies Concept—Social Darwinism

I would include this concept because it played an important part in justifying aggressive western imperialism—Darwin's theory of natural selection was applied to competition between nations, with the idea that the strongest (industrialized Europeans) should virtually conquer weak (non-industrialized) peoples.

(4) Metaphor/Analogy/Historical Parallel

Believing in Social Darwinism is like believing that the whole of life is a footrace where there is only one prize and the prize goes to the fittest and swiftest runner. This analogy is appropriate because Europeans saw themselves as the most advanced people in the world, giving them the right to conquer and control other people and places.

(5) Questions for Class Discussion

- What role did economic factors have in the partition of Africa among European powers?

- What effect have colonial boundaries had on life in postcolonial Africa? (Geography)

Scoring Commentary

- To earn a score of 3, the response must demonstrate a clear understanding of relevant subject matter. This test taker does so clearly for Question 1. The selected topic, the scramble for Africa, certainly is central to the unit. The test taker also includes important specific information about the topic: the time frame of the historical event (the end of the nineteenth century), the players involved (the industrialized European powers), the central action (the carving up of a continent), and its significance (consequences that persist to today).

- Question 2 requires merely the titles of two additional subject matter topics. The test taker has chosen two that are relevant to the central topic and yet are distinct from it and from each other.

- In Question 3, the test taker further demonstrates understanding of the subject by choosing a relevant social studies concept: Social Darwinism. To receive full credit, the response must explain why the concept is important and therefore deserves inclusion in the lesson. This test taker notes that Social Darwinism was used as a pseudoscientific justification for aggressive imperialism.

- Question 4 asks for a metaphor, analogy, or historical parallel that would be useful for clarifying the concept identified in Question 3, plus an explanation for the one chosen. The test taker has chosen an appropriate metaphor—a footrace—and gives an adequate explanation for how it applies to the ideology of Social Darwinism and the behavior of the colonial powers.

- Question 5 asks for two questions that will provoke class discussion and require students to use more than factual recall. Both of the questions meet this standard and show the test taker's understanding of the historical context of imperialism. As required, the test taker provides at least one question that makes explicit connections between history and one or more social science disciplines and identifies which discipline. In this case, the second question is related to geography, as the test taker notes parenthetically. The test taker might also have noted that the first question is related to economics, but for full credit only one question needs to have this relationship.

Sample response that received a score of 1

(1) Subject Matter Topic 1—Europe's Colonies in America

Students need to know how Europe became imperialistic with America and put its values and culture in the American colonies

(2) Subject Matter Topic 2—How Europe's imperialism over America spread to other regions of the world

Subject Matter Topic 3—Reasons why Europe decided to end Colonialism

(3) Social Studies Concept—"Domination"

This concept reflects these subjects because Imperialism and Colonialism were about the domination of one country by another.

(4) Metaphor/Analogy/Historical Parallel

Domination is like a bully on a playground who won't let others do anything without his approval.

(5) Questions for Class Discussion

1. Who was the first and most successful Imperial and Colonial country, and when and why?

2. Which country or countries were most successful in rebelling against imperialism?

Scoring Commentary

- A response earns a score of 1 if it demonstrates a weak understanding of the subject matter and pedagogy and provides inappropriate or little support. In responding to Question 1, this test taker suggests a topic that is adequate. It would have been better if the test taker had specified whether the topic was about colonies in North and South America or only those in what is now the United States. More serious is the failure of the response to explain why this subject matter topic is central to the unit.

- The two additional subject matter topics proposed for Question 2 are generally satisfactory, although the first of these ("How Europe's imperialism over America spread to other regions of the world") is too sweeping in scope to be effective as a topic.

- The concept of "domination" proposed for Question 3 is an appropriate choice because it is important in the definition of imperialism, but the test taker's justification for using it is inadequate. He or she gives no historical context that would explain why imperialism (or colonialism) was different from any other historical domination of one country or region by another. Throughout the test taker's responses, the terms *imperialism* and *colonialism* are used interchangeably, showing an imprecise understanding of the distinctions between the terms.

- The metaphor that the test taker proposes for Question 4—the playground bully—is appropriate to some extent, but the test taker's explanation is clearly inadequate. He or she could have written that imperialism involved aggression and control and often enriched the dominating state (analogous to extorting lunch money), but instead control is the only detail given (the bully "won't let others do anything without his approval").

- Both of the questions that the test taker proposes for Question 5 could provoke a lot of classroom discussion—probably too much, since both are quite unfocused. To answer either question, students would first have to define criteria for what it means to be "successful." This task would raise a lot of difficult issues, such as whether the independence of a troubled country like Pakistan or Myanmar has been a "success," and students would be distracted from the central topic, imperialism and colonialism. Question 5 requires that at least one of the proposed questions relate history to a social science discipline, and that the test taker identify the discipline. Neither of these two questions has an obvious relationship to another discipline. Conceivably, definitions of success could be linked to economics in the first or to political science in the second, but the test taker does not point out any such connection.

In conclusion

Whatever approach you take to organizing your response, the important consideration is that your answer be thorough, complete, and detailed. You need to be certain to do the following:

- Answer all five questions related to each case study.

- Give reasons for your answers, where required.

- Demonstrate subject-specific knowledge and knowledge of pedagogy in your answer.

Chapter 11
Practice Test—*Social Studies: Pedagogy*

▶ ▶ ▶ ▶ ▶ ▶ ▶ ▶ ▶ ▶ ▶ ▶

Now that you have worked through strategies and preparation relating to the *Social Studies: Pedagogy* test, you should take the following practice test. This test is an actual Praxis test, now retired. You will probably find it helpful to simulate actual testing conditions, giving yourself 60 minutes to work on the questions. You can use the lined answer pages provided if you wish.

Keep in mind that the test you take at an actual administration will have different questions. You should not expect your level of performance to be exactly the same as when you take the test at an actual administration, since numerous factors affect a person's performance in any given testing situation.

When you have finished the practice questions, you can read through the sample responses with scorer annotations in chapter 12.

Professional Assessments for Beginning Teachers ®

TEST NAME:

Social Studies:

Pedagogy (0084)

Time—60 minutes

2 Questions

CASE STUDY I

Note: For Case Study I, you are to select a course and a unit of study and answer five separate but related questions. All five questions in Case Study I are presented together immediately below to help you organize your thinking. The five questions are then repeated, with space provided for your answers, on pages 133–142. For 1–3 in Case Study I, an example of an appropriate response is also provided below. (These examples of appropriate responses are <u>not</u> repeated on pages 133–142.)

<u>Option A</u>

Course: United States History

Unit: Westward Expansion

<u>Option B</u>

Course: World History

Unit: The Renaissance

Select <u>one</u> of the two options above (Option A <u>or</u> Option B). Assume that you are in the process of developing a two-week unit of study. In planning this two-week unit, complete (1–5) below. Do <u>not</u> present a full plan for the two-week unit.

NOTE: For the purposes of this test, a "Subject Matter Topic" means a social studies topic that refers to a specific subject or time period; a "Social Studies Concept" is an idea that can be applied to various subjects and time periods.

Central Subject Matter Topic

(10%) 1. Identify a subject matter topic that you consider <u>central</u> for teaching the unit. (EXAMPLE: For a unit on "European Colonization of the Americas," one possible central subject matter topic would be "The Interaction Between Europeans and Native Peoples.")

Briefly explain why you consider this subject matter topic <u>central</u> for teaching the unit.

Additional Subject Matter Topics

(5%) 2. Identify <u>two additional</u> subject matter topics that you think are critical for teaching the unit. (EXAMPLE: For a unit on "European Colonization of the Americas," two possible additional subject matter topics would be "European National Rivalries" and "Motivations of Individual European Colonists.")

The two additional subject matter topics should be <u>clearly distinct</u> from each other and from the subject matter topic you have identified in (1) above. (Note: You only need to <u>identify</u> the subject matter topics, although these topics must be stated clearly.)

Social Studies Concept

(10%) 3. Identify a key social studies concept you would include in this unit that is essential to one or more of the subject matter topics you have identified in (1) and (2) above. (EXAMPLE: For a unit on "European Colonization of the Americas," one possible social studies concept essential to "The Interaction Between Europeans and Native Peoples," a subject matter topic given above, would be "Ethnocentrism.")

Briefly explain why you would include this social studies concept and how it is essential to one or more of the subject matter topics you have identified.

Metaphor/Analogy/Historical Parallel

(15%) 4. Describe a metaphor, analogy, or historical parallel that you might use to help students understand the social studies concept you have identified in (3) above.

Briefly explain why the metaphor, analogy, or historical parallel you have described is appropriate.

Questions for Class Discussion

(10%) 5. Develop <u>two</u> questions for class discussion that would help students understand one or more of the subject matter topics or the social studies concept you have identified in (1), (2), or (3) above.

CASE STUDY I CONTINUED

Both questions <u>must require students to use cognitive abilities above the level of factual recall</u>; that is, analysis, application, evaluation, or synthesis. <u>At least one</u> of the questions must also make <u>explicit connections between history and one or more social science disciplines</u>.

Be sure to identify the discipline(s) to which you are making connections.

Central Subject Matter Topic

(10%) 1.   Identify a subject matter topic that you consider <u>central</u> for teaching the unit.

Briefly explain why you consider this subject matter topic <u>central</u> for teaching the unit.

Write your choice of Option A or B here: _____

Write your response to Case Study I, (1) here.

Central subject matter topic: _____

_____

_____

_____

_____

_____

Explanation: _____

_____

_____

_____

_____

_____

_____

_____

_____

_____

_____

_____

_____

_____

CASE STUDY I CONTINUED

Additional Subject Matter Topics

(5%) 2. Identify <u>two</u> additional subject matter topics that you think are critical for teaching the unit.

The two additional subject matter topics should be <u>clearly distinct</u> from each other and from the subject matter topic you have identified in (1) above. (Note: You only need to <u>identify</u> the subject matter topics, although these topics must be stated clearly.)

Write your response to Case Study I, (2) here.

First topic:

Second topic:

CASE STUDY I CONTINUED

Social Studies Concept

(10%) 3. Identify a key social studies concept you would include in this unit that is essential to one or more of the subject matter topics you have identified in 1 and 2 above.

Briefly explain why you would include this social studies concept and how it is essential to one or more of the subject matter topics you have identified.

Write your response to Case Study I, (3) here.

Social studies concept:

Explanation:

CASE STUDY I CONTINUED

Metaphor/Analogy/Historical Parallel

(15%) 4. Describe a metaphor, analogy, or historical parallel that you might use to help students understand the social studies concept you have identified in 3 above.

Briefly explain why the metaphor, analogy, or historical parallel you have described is appropriate.

Write your response to Case Study I, (4) here.

Metaphor/analogy/historical parallel:

_____

_____

_____

_____

_____

_____

Explanation:

_____

_____

_____

_____

_____

_____

_____

_____

_____

_____

_____

_____

_____

_____

CASE STUDY I CONTINUED

Questions for Class Discussion

(10%) 5. Develop two questions for class discussion that would help students understand one or more of the subject matter topics or the social studies concept you have identified in 1, 2, or 3 above.

Both questions must require students to use cognitive abilities above the level of factual recall; that is, analysis, application, evaluation, or synthesis. At least one of the questions must also make explicit connections between history and one or more social science disciplines.

Be sure to identify the discipline(s) to which you are making connections.

Write your response to Case Study I, (5) here.

First question:

Second question:

CASE STUDY II

Note: For Case Study II, you are to select a course and a unit of study and answer five separate but related questions. All five questions in Case Study II are presented together immediately below to help you organize your thinking. The five questions are then repeated, with space provided for your answers, on pages 145–154. For 1–3 in Case Study II, an example of an appropriate response is also provided below. (These examples of appropriate responses are not repeated on pages 145–154.)

<u>Option A</u>

Course: Government

Unit: Freedom of Speech

<u>Option B</u>

Course: Economics

Unit: Unemployment

<u>Option C</u>

Course: Geography

Unit: Economic and Cultural Geography of Latin America

Select <u>one</u> of the three options above (Option A or Option B or Option C). Assume that you are developing a lesson for a single class period of 40–45 minutes within the unit you have selected. In planning this lesson, answer 1–5 below. Do <u>not</u> present a full lesson plan.

Lesson

(10%) 1.　Identify a topic to be the focus of this lesson.

Explain why this particular topic warrants a full class period within the unit.

Objective

(10%) 2.　State a primary objective for this lesson. (An objective identifies a <u>measurable or observable</u> student outcome.)

Teaching Strategy

(15%) 3.　Identify a teaching strategy that is consistent with the objective you have identified in (2) above.

Explain why this teaching strategy is appropriate for this objective.

Evaluation: Essay Question

(5%) 4.　Write one clear examination question to evaluate students' level of achievement <u>for the objective you have identified in (2) above</u>. The question you present should require students to use cognitive abilities above the level of factual recall.

Another Method of Evaluation

(10%) 5.　Describe another method of evaluation (<u>not</u> an examination) that you could use to evaluate students' level of achievement <u>for the same objective</u>.

Explain why this method of evaluation is appropriate for the objective.

CASE STUDY II CONTINUED

Lesson

(10%) 1. Identify a topic to be the focus of this lesson.

Explain why this particular topic warrants a full class period within the unit.

Write your choice of Option A <u>or</u> B <u>or</u> C here:_____

Write your response to Case Study II, (1) here

Topic for lesson:

Explanation:

CASE STUDY II CONTINUED

Objective

(10%) 2.   State a primary objective for this lesson. (An objective identifies a <u>measurable or observable</u> student outcome.)

Write your response to Case Study II, (2) here.

Objective:

CASE STUDY II CONTINUED

Teaching Strategy

(15%) 3. Identify a teaching strategy that is consistent with the objective you have identified in (2) above.

Explain why this teaching strategy is appropriate for this objective.

Write your response to Case Study II, (3) here.

Teaching strategy:

Explanation:

CASE STUDY II CONTINUED

Evaluation: Essay Question

(5%) 4. Write one clear essay examination question to evaluate students' level of achievement <u>for the objective you have identified in (2) above</u>. The question you present should require students to use cognitive abilities above the level of factual recall.

Write your response to Case Study II, (4) here.

Essay question:

_____

_____

_____

_____

_____

_____

_____

_____

_____

_____

_____

_____

_____

_____

_____

_____

_____

_____

_____

_____

_____

CASE STUDY II CONTINUED

Another Method of Evaluation

(10%) 5. Describe another method of evaluation (<u>not</u> an examination) that you could use to evaluate students' level of achievement <u>for the same objective</u>.

Explain why this method of evaluation is appropriate for the objective.

Write your response to Case Study II, (5) here.

Another method of evaluation:

Explanation:

Chapter 12
Sample Responses and How They Were Scored—
Social Studies: Pedagogy

▶ ▶ ▶ ▶ ▶ ▶ ▶ ▶ ▶ ▶ ▶ ▶

This chapter presents actual sample responses to the questions in the practice test and explanations for the scores they received.

As discussed in chapter 3, each question on the *Social Studies: Pedagogy* test is scored on a scale from 0 to 3. The General Scoring Guide used to score these questions is reprinted here for your convenience.

Score	Comment
3	Accurate and complete.

- Demonstrates a clear understanding of relevant subject matter and pedagogy
- Provides appropriate, accurate, and complete explanations and/or supporting information

2 Mostly accurate and complete

- Demonstrates an adequate understanding of relevant subject matter and pedagogy
- Provides mostly appropriate, accurate, and complete explanations and/or supporting information

1 Inaccurate and incomplete

- Demonstrates a weak understanding of subject matter and pedagogy
- Provides inappropriate and/or little support (when needed)

0 Completely inaccurate or inappropriate, blank, off topic, or only a restatement of the prompt

Case Study I

There are five questions for Case Study I; the total number of points that a response can receive from each scorer is 15.

We will now look at five actual responses to Case Study I and see how the scoring guide above was used to rate each response.

Sample response that earned a score of 15

Option A

Question 1

Central subject matter topic: The United States government's justification of expanding west.

Explanation: I consider this topic central for teaching the unit because it looks at the motivating factors of westward expansion. It also looks at the reasoning and justification, such as national security, economics, & self defense, which brought expansion to fruition.

Question 2

First topic: Effects of Expansion, which would deal with how the United States treated various ethnic groups in expansion west, notably the Native Americans & the Mexicans. Expansion west came at the great expense of these two groups.

Second topic: Life on the frontier, which would look primarily at what motivated individuals to move west. It would examine lives of famous like Daniel Boone, Davy Crockett, and the Donner Party to the lives of miners, Indians, and women on the frontier. It would paint a picture of hardship & perseverance using primary documents like letters & contracts.

Question 3

Social studies concept: Manifest Destiny is a concept central to the unit & subject matter topics of both of the effects of Expansion & the spirit in which it was undertaken, in life on the frontier.

Explanation: I would include this concept because it is the root of westward expansion, justifying expansion as a God Given right of Americans. As such, it is seen as essential to national security and pride in the country to expand its boundaries coastline to coastline.

Question 4

Metaphor/analogy/historical parallel: "The End Justifies the Means" is an appropriate metaphor for the unit. It would help the students think in terms of costs & benefits.

Explanation: It is appropriate because students would think in terms of costs and benefits and be confronted immediately w/ a moral dilemma— "Did the end justify the means?" and "Was Westward expansion justified— to the Mexicans? To the Indians? To Americans? "Would you undo the grains of Manifest Destiny & Westward expansion?

Sample Responses to Case Study I, continued

Question 5

First question: Weighing the costs & benefits of Westward expansion, give 3 reasons why it was or wasn't justified & support your statement with facts.

Second question: Give 3 reasons why the Polk Administration wanted to expand the country and explain the economic, social or political outcomes of each.

Scoring Commentary

Question 1: (Score of 3) The test taker provides a subject matter topic that is appropriate for inclusion in a two-week unit because the topic focuses on a central issue, as opposed to trivial or tangential issues or isolated facts. There is a persuasive explanation of why the topic chosen is critical to the unit.

Question 2: (Score of 3) Two subject matter topics are mentioned, both of which are critical and clearly distinct both from one another and from the topic in Question 1.

Question 3: (Score of 3) The test taker mentions a key concept that is essential to the subject matter topic identified in Question 1.

Question 4: (Score of 3) The test taker provides a clear metaphor that contributes to students' understanding of the social studies concept identified in Question 3. A persuasive explanation for the appropriateness of the metaphor is provided.

Question 5: (Score of 3) Both questions would help students understand the topics and concept, and both require more than factual recall. Question 2 makes explicit interdisciplinary connections.

Sample response that earned a score of 12

<u>Option A</u>

Question 1

Central subject matter topic: Reasons for westward expansion.

Explanation: Westward expansion was important for many reasons: lands, riches, and resources. Students should know why the west was valuable for exploration and movement.

Question 2

First topic: What effects did moving westward have on the native Indians.

Second topic: Important discoveries that people found in the west.

Question 3

Social studies concept: Exploration

Explanation: I would include this concept because this is a main reason why the colonialists moved west. It is essential because it is an act that the people did and were described as.

Question 4

Metaphor/analogy/historical parallel: Exploration is like the NASA, where they are trying to find new planets and galaxies with the launching of the telescope Galileo and the launchings of the space shuttles.

Explanation: Using NASA is important because it is currently trying to find out what lies beyond our solar system. In addition, NASA is trying to find other life forms and planets that might be useful to earth. Similarly, westward expansion in the past dealt with finding new lands and resources. For instance, the California Gold Rush and the buffalo.

Question 5

First question: What resources were discovered that pushed for westward expansion.

Second question: What was the physical characteristics of the land in the following states like: California, Oregon, Nevada, Texas, Oklahoma and Utah.

Scoring Commentary

Question 1: (Score of 3) The test taker has chosen a subject matter topic that is appropriate for inclusion in a two-week unit because the topic focuses on a central issue. The explanation of why the topic chosen is critical to the unit is persuasive.

Question 2: (Score of 3) Two subject matter topics that are critical and clearly distinct both from one another and from the topic in Question 1 are provided.

Question 3: (Score of 2) The test taker provides a key concept, but an inadequate explanation.

Question 4: (Score of 3) The test taker describes a clear historical parallel that clarifies and contributes to the students' understanding of the concept identified in Question 3. A persuasive explanation is given for the appropriateness of the historical parallel.

Question 5: (Score of 1) Two questions are listed, but neither requires more than factual recall, and neither makes an explicit interdisciplinary connection.

Sample Responses to Case Study I, continued

Sample response that earned a score of 12

<u>Option B</u>

Question 1

Central subject matter topic: How the increase in trade allowed people of the Renaissance to question their surroundings and themselves.

Explanation: Students too often take for granted their surroundings and do not question why things occurred. I would try to use the Renaissance to show how trade affected Italy and allowed Italians because of the money that trade provided allowed them to get a better education. At the same time this free time allowed them to question their surroundings and their own existence. This allowed them to paint in perspective, expand philosophy and thought, and question political reality.

Question 2

First topic: I believe it is important to have the student identify and compare art from the Renaissance from periods of art from the Egyptians to the Middle Ages.

Second topic: I would also like the students to read and apply Machiavelli's "The Prince" to modern day politics and government.

Question 3

Social studies concept: The role of government, and how individuals action shape government actions.

Explanation: I would like the students to understand some of the philosophies behind current politics. By having the students bring in current event articles and become aware of political reality. When the students are able to identify some of the aspects of the current political landscape then to introduce and discuss Machiavelli's view of politics in Italy during the Renaissance. I would like the students to pull out certain themes from Machiavelli's book, such as, any goal to achieve power, appeasement of the people, fearing or loving leaders. Then once the students can identify Machiavelli's ideas and current politics to compare those ideas to see if they are still practiced by today's leaders.

Question 4

Metaphor/analogy/historical parallel: Again I would have the students look at current day politics. This has included in the past to look at political campaigns to compare what politicians say to get power. I then have the students gauge the purpose of their promises especially after they have read Machiavelli.

Explanation: I think it is important for students to be critical of government, so they can be more aware and make knowledgeable choices as voters and as possible leaders. I would like them to challenge what is said and to be active in government.

Question 5

First question: How is the role of leaders during the Renaissance different or similar to the leader of today?

-Role of government-

Second question: What role should individuals take to make government accountable?

-Role of individuals in government-

Scoring Commentary

Question 1: (Score of 3) The key subject matter topic is appropriate for inclusion in a two-week unit because the topic focuses on a central issue. The test taker provides a persuasive explanation of why the topic chosen is critical to the unit.

Question 2: (Score of 3) The two subject matter topics are critical and clearly distinct both from one another and from the topic in Question 1.

Question 3: (Score of 2) The test taker provides a key concept, but it is not stated specifically as a concept. There is an adequate explanation relating to the second topic in Question 2.

Question 4: (Score of 2) The historical parallel is vague, but an adequate explanation is provided.

Question 5: (Score of 2) The test taker provides two questions, the first of which would help students understand the subject matter concept identified in Question 3.

Sample Responses to Case Study I, continued

Sample response that earned a score of 10

Option A

Question 1

Central subject matter topic: The effect that Western Expansion had for the United States of America. (then & now)

Explanation: Students should be able to not only describe the significance of such a historical event, but the effects of it as well. So much learning in social studies is fragmented. Students need to see the connections that Western expansion has on their lives today. These connections will give the students a reason and a desire to learn about the material.

Question 2

First topic: Reasons for western expansion. Before the effects are discussed, students should know why people risked their lives and their family to make such a journey.

Second topic: Demographics of the people that moved west. Students should identify the types of people that moved. This would add more texture to the unit and make the learning more personal to the student. Students can make connections with their cultural background as well.

Question 3

Social studies concept: Obstacles of Western Expansion

Explanation: It would be important for the students to realize the obstacles faced in such a journey. Students could relate their own goals & obstacles with those of the pioneers. They could realize that it is important to hold on your dreams even if a difficult path lies ahead. Western Expansion does not seem as significant if the students do not understand the obstacles that were faced.

Question 4

Metaphor/analogy/historical parallel: 1. Goals/Dreams—how to achieve them? 2. Space Exploration.

Explanation: 1. Students could use Western Expansion as an analogy for their own dreams and the obstacles they will face. 2. The people that made such a voyage were travelling in a new and dangerous territory. The same could be said for space exploration. Students can relate what they know about space exploration to Western Expansion. Space Explorers risked a great deal in order to discover new territory. What were the similarities and differences of space explorers and those that moved west.

Question 5

First question: What are the similarities and differences between space explorers and those that took part in Western Expansion?

Students will need to analyze the people and their motivation for western expansion and apply this to space exploration. Students are moving beyond simple recall and must apply their knowledge to the current time.

Second question: What economical and geographical reasons encouraged Western expansion?

Students will be evaluating the 1. economical & geographical reasons for Western expansion. Money, climate, and land were some of the reasons for expansion.

Scoring Commentary

Question 1: (Score of 1) The test taker provides a subject matter topic that may be appropriate, but the explanation of why the topic chosen is critical to the unit is inadequate.

Question 2: (Score of 3) The two subject matter topics are critical and clearly distinct both from one another and from the topic in Question 1.

Question 3: (Score of 1) The test taker provides an additional appropriate subject matter topic, not a concept.

Question 4: (Score of 3) Although Question 3 was not a concept, this response provides a metaphor that would help students understand the idea identified in Question 3. It provides a persuasive explanation for the appropriateness of the metaphor.

Question 5: (Score of 2) The test taker provides two questions, one of which would help students understand one of the topics in Question 2.

Sample Responses to Case Study I, continued

Sample response that earned a score of 7

<u>Option A</u>

Question 1

Central subject matter topic: The movement that affected many people

Explanation: The westward expansion involved people from the North, South, Native Indians, and Mexicans.

In the North, people were free while preserving the Union. They wanted to clean the "ills" of society by providing jobs and homes. Meanwhile, in the South "slavery was a positive good." White Southerners wanted to keep their slaves for labor. At the same time many slaves tried to escape to the North to be free.

The Northerners kept moving west taking trading, and making deals for the lands that were already occupied by the Native Indians. Their impacted the native Indians especially when they were placed in reservations.

Then the Mexicans were affected by White Northerners has they settled on Mexican land.

Question 2

First topic: The battle of the Native Indians.

Second topic: Gold nuggets found in California.

Question 3

Social studies concept: Ethnocentrism

Explanation: Ethnocentrism is last in describing the subject matter. "The movement that affected many people" because the Northerners who moved west brought to their (Northerner) values, beliefs, and laws that affected the natives by changing their lifestyles.

Question 4

Metaphor/analogy/historical parallel: The white man's land.

Explanation: The white Northerners were the greatest influence in the Westward expansion. Like, religion, culture, and behaviors

Question 5

First question: Why were the Northerners so influential in the westward expansion?

Second question: Where were the Native Indians placed when white Northerners invaded their land?

Scoring Commentary

Question 1: (Score of 2) The test taker provides a subject matter topic that is appropriate, but focuses on themes that are important though not necessarily central. An adequate explanation is provided.

Question 2: (Score of 1) The first subject matter topic chosen is not clearly distinct from the topic in Question 1; the second subject matter topic chosen is not critical.

Question 3: (Score of 2) The test taker provides a key concept but an inadequate explanation.

Question 4: (Score of 1) The test taker provides a metaphor that is unclear, and does not contribute to the students' understanding of the concept identified in Question 3. The explanation is inadequate.

Question 5: (Score of 1) Two questions are provided, neither of which relates clearly to the topics or the concept. Neither makes an explicit interdisciplinary connection, and only one question requires more than factual recall.

Case Study II

There are five questions for Case Study II; the total number of points that a response can receive from each scorer is 15. We will now look at five responses to Case Study II and see how the scoring guide above was used to rate each response.

Sample response that earned a score of 15

Option A

Question 1

Central subject matter topic: Schneck vs. The United States, supreme court case 1919.

Explanation: This case would look at how our 1st amendment right to freedom of speech was tested, in this case in a time of war. It would explain the weight of this right between individual freedom & national security & the greater good.

Sample Responses to Case Study II, continued

Question 2

Objectives: At the end of this lesson, the students will be able to identify 3 reasons why free speech is sometimes dangerous & should have limits.

Question 3

Teaching strategy: Show a video of the KKK marches & the ensuing riots, because this is something all students can identify with. Follow up w/ primary documents from Schneck vs. U.S. with an inquiry lesson—"Why did the government arrest Schneck?"

Explanation: The video would be something the kids have had exposure to. The Inquiry would make them curious to read primary documents.

Question 4

Essay question: Discuss the Schneck case and explain 3 reasons why his right to free speech should or should not have been protected.

Question 5

Another method of evaluation: Socratic Method, or questioning using documented evidence in addition to the students' own political views & personal experience.

Explanation: Socratic method would get the students involved in intellectual discourse on the 1st Amendment. It would foster analytical & oral skills as well as research, reading, & life skills like courtesy & listening to others & patients.

Scoring Commentary

Question 1: (Score of 3) The test taker provides a topic that is central to the unit and appropriate for a lesson of 40 to 45 minutes. There is a sound explanation of why the topic is an appropriate focus for the lesson.

Question 2: (Score of 3) The stated objective is appropriate and clearly identifies a measurable or observable student outcome.

Question 3: (Score of 3) The test taker identifies an appropriate teaching strategy for the objective chosen in Question 2.

Question 4: (Score of 3) The test taker provides an essay question that is appropriate to the objective stated in Question 2, clearly states what is expected of the student, and requires more than factual recall.

Question 5: (Score of 3) The method of evaluation is appropriate to evaluate students' level of achievement for the objective; a persuasive explanation is provided.

Sample response that earned a score of 11

<u>Option C</u>

Question 1

Topic for lesson: New Imperialism in Latin America

Explanation: Students need to know that America as well as European powers have gotten around the Monroe Doctrine and the Roosevelt Collary (sp?) by hearing strong presences, influences in the economy, political & social life of the LA countries by sometimes underhanded or overtly aggressive tactics that still greatly resemble imperialism, i.e. supporting political opposition w/ money & warfare or forcing countries to provide best trade prices.

Question 2

Objective: Students will be able to chart various ways America & European powers have a great deal of influence in LA countries into three categories —political, economical, & social.

Question 3

Teaching strategy: Role playing.

Explanation: By dividing the class into three separate entities—European or American power, the LA gov't, the people of LA gov't. We can explore a possible situation & examine their reaction. I would use a situation that really happened like the Contra Affair & have each entity respond what their action would be.

Question 4

Essay question: Choose a LA country & explain how America or European powers have a great influence in their political economy & social life.

Question 5

Another method of evaluation: Have students construct a chart.

Explanation:

Sample Responses to Case Study II, continued

Scoring Commentary

Question 1: (Score of 3) The test taker provides a topic that is central to the unit and appropriate for a lesson of 40 to 45 minutes. There is a sound explanation of why the topic is an appropriate focus for the lesson.

Question 2: (Score of 3) The test taker provides an appropriate objective that clearly identifies a measurable or observable student outcome.

Question 3: (Score of 1) The teaching strategy described is not clearly related to the objective.

Question 4: (Score of 3) The essay question is appropriate to the objective and clearly states what is expected of the student.

Question 5: (Score of 1) The contents of the alternative method of evaluation are not clear. No explanation is given.

Sample response that earned a score of 9

Option A

Question 1

Topic for lesson: How does freedom of speech on our lives? [What opportunities does it provide us?]

Explanation: This is a broad topic, but I feel that it is essential for students to see how it influences their lives. It also is important to illustrate how it makes this country a unique place to live and the opportunities that it offers.

Question 2

Objective: Evaluate the influences of the 1st Amendment.

Question 3

Teaching strategy: Students could read about an incident where a citizen in another country was not allowed freedom of speech—perhaps jailed for what they spoke out against. ie. Nelson Mandela.

Explanation: This would allow students to see the difference between our opportunities in their country and those from other countries.

Question 4

Essay question: Discuss the advantages (benefits) that Americans have with freedom of speech.

Question 5

Another method of evaluation: Role play of a situation an incident where someone did not have access to freedom of speech to a person who does.

Explanation: Allow students to use an alternative form to express the benefits.

Scoring Commentary

Question 1: (Score of 2) The test taker provides a topic that is germane to the unit, as well as an adequate explanation.

Question 2: (Score of 1) The test taker provides an objective that is not related to the topic in Question 1 and that cannot be measured or observed.

Question 3: (Score of 3) The test taker mentions a teaching strategy that is related to the topic of the lesson. Even though the objective is inappropriate, the topic is germane and there is a persuasive explanation for why the teaching strategy is appropriate for this specific lesson.

Question 4: (Score of 2) The essay question is mostly appropriate for the lesson but it is somewhat unclear as to what is expected of the student.

Question 5: (Score of 1) The alternative method of evaluation is unclear, and an inadequate explanation is provided.

Sample response that earned a score of 7

Option B

Question 1

Topic for lesson: Different types of unemployment

Explanation: Being that unemployment is an important issue in today's society, it is imperative that students understand and recognize the different types of unemployment and how it affects them.

Question 2

Objective: At the end of this lesson, students will be able to:

1. Define unemployment

2. Identify the different types of unemployment

Sample Responses to Case Study II, continued

Question 3

Teaching strategy:

1. Have students read chapter on unemployment.

2. Divide the students in five groups and have them list the key identifiers of each type of unemployment.

3. After the students have been in their groups for a total of 15 minutes, have them share & correlate their findings to the other groups.

4. Have students return to their individual seating and distribute worksheet with examples on it. Have them match the correct type of unemployment to each example.

Explanation:

Question 4

Essay question:

Question 5

Another method of evaluation: Assign students to groups and have them go to five different companies and ask them questions pertaining to the types of unemployment we have just covered.

Explanation: This activity will re-introduce the computer we have covered and give them a personal

Scoring Commentary

Question 1: (Score of 2) The topic is germane to the unit; an adequate explanation is provided.

Question 2: (Score of 3) The test taker provides an objective that clearly identifies a measurable or observable student outcome.

Question 3: (Score of 1) Although the teaching strategy is appropriate, no explanation is given as to why this strategy is appropriate.

Question 4: (Score of 0) Blank.

Question 5: (Score of 1) The response is not a method of evaluation but an alternative teaching strategy. The explanation is inadequate.

Sample response that earned a score of 5

Option C

Question 1

Topic for lesson: Latin America—where is it located, why is it important to the world economy, and what are its people like? (An overview)

Explanation: This class period will be an overview of Latin America and what to expect in this unit of study.

Question 2

Objective: Students will be able to locate Latin America and identify its major cities.

Question 3

Teaching strategy: Lecture/Discussion

Explanation: Present facts and discuss with students to ensure understanding.

Question 4

Essay question:

Question 5

Another method of evaluation: Create a model or an original map.

Explanation: An original, creative work.

Scoring Commentary

Question 1: (Score of 2) The test taker provides a topic that is germane to the unit but may exceed time limits of a lesson of 40 to 45 minutes. There is an adequate explanation of why the topic is an appropriate focus for the lesson.

Question 2: (Score of 1) The objective is not related to the topic of the lesson in Question 1.

Question 3: (Score of 1) The test taker identifies a teaching strategy not specifically related to the topic of the lesson. There is an inadequate explanation for why this teaching strategy is appropriate.

Question 4: (Score of 0) Blank.

Question 5: (Score of 1) The test taker provides an alternative method of evaluation that is unclear and would not be adequate to evaluate students' level of achievement for the objective. The explanation is inadequate.

Chapter 13

Preparing for the *Social Studies: Interpretation and Analysis* Test

► ► ► ► ► ► ► ► ► ► ► ►

The goal of this chapter is to provide you with strategies for preparing for the questions on the *Social Studies: Interpretation and Analysis* test. Because the content of this test overlaps with the content of two other tests included in this study guide, you will find no separate listing of books and other materials appropriate for studying for the *Social Studies: Interpretation and Analysis* test, nor is there a separate practice test. Instead, this chapter explains how to use **other chapters in this book** to prepare for the test.

Introduction to the Question Types

The *Social Studies: Interpretation and Analysis* test is intended to assess whether you have the knowledge and skills necessary to be a beginning teacher of social studies in a secondary school.

The test is composed of two parts that are weighted equally.

Part I

Part I consists of five two-part short-answer questions that require reading and interpreting social studies materials, drawing inferences from such materials, and relating these materials to knowledge of the individual fields in social studies. Material presented for interpretation can take the form of a map, chart, graph, table, cartoon, diagram, quotation, or an excerpt from a document.

The first part of each question requires identifying or demonstrating comprehension of the material presented. The second part requires interpreting or explaining the material, drawing inferences about it, and/or relating it to knowledge beyond information given in the question and stimulus.

You probably should spend about 10 to 12 minutes on each question.

Part II

Part II consists of two equally weighted essay questions that require analysis of contemporary and historical issues, understanding of interdisciplinary relationships and fundamental social studies concepts, and synthesis and integration of information within an analytical essay.

One of the two essay questions contains United States subject matter; the other, world subject matter. One emphasizes historical issues; the other, contemporary issues. At least one incorporates stimulus material (e.g., a map, chart, cartoon, diagram, quotation, or an excerpt from a document), and at least one emphasizes bringing outside knowledge to bear on the interpretation of the material.

You probably should spend about 30 minutes on each of these questions.

What to Study

This test covers the following content areas:

I. History: United States and World

II. Social Science: Government, Geography, and Economics

III. Social Studies Analysis: United States

IV. Social Studies Analysis: World

Chapters 4 and 7 contain lists of useful books and other materials that can help you improve your understanding of these subjects. You probably will also want to review textbooks and notes from courses you've taken.

Understanding What the Questions Are Asking

Part I questions

To understand the kinds of questions that appear in Part I of this test, look at the section in **chapter 7** called "Understanding What the Questions Are Asking." That chapter describes the *Social Studies: Interpretation of Materials* test, but what it says is equally true for Part I of the *Social Studies: Interpretation and Analysis* test. By reading this section of chapter 7 you'll see the following:

- An example of the kinds of questions you can expect to encounter
- Analysis of what the questions are asking
- Tips on planning and writing your response
- Sample responses
- Scorers' comments on the sample responses

Part II questions

The section in **chapter 4** called "Understanding What the Questions Are Asking" will help you understand the kinds of questions that appear in Part II of this test. What that chapter says about the *Social Studies: Analytical Essays* test applies equally well to Part II of the *Social Studies: Interpretation and Analysis* test. Chapter 4 shows you the following:

- An example of the kinds of questions you can expect to encounter
- Analysis of what the questions are asking
- Tips on planning and writing your response
- Sample responses
- Scorers' comments on the sample responses

Taking a Practice Test

Taking the *Social Studies: Interpretation and Analysis* test is equivalent to taking the *Social Studies: Interpretation of Materials* test and the *Social Studies: Analytical Essays* test back to back. Therefore, you can simulate taking the *Social Studies: Interpretation and Analysis* test by taking the practice test in chapter 8 followed immediately by the practice test in chapter 5. Allow yourself one hour to work on each of the two practice tests, for a session of two hours total.

Then read chapters 9 and 6 to see examples of how real test takers answered the practice questions. Note what scores the sample responses earned and read the comments the scorers made in explaining these scores. Compare your own responses to these examples and decide what you did right and wrong. Think about how you might improve your responses to earn additional points from the scorers.

Chapter 14
Are You Ready? Last-Minute Tips

▶ ▶ ▶ ▶ ▶ ▶ ▶ ▶ ▶ ▶ ▶ ▶

Checklist

Complete this checklist to determine whether you're ready to take the test.

❑ Do you know the testing requirements for your field in the state(s) where you plan to teach?

❑ Have you followed all of the test registration procedures?

❑ Do you know the topics covered in each test you plan to take?

❑ Have you reviewed any textbooks, class notes, and course readings related to the topics covered?

❑ Do you know how long the test will take and the number of questions it contains? Have you considered how you will pace your work?

❑ Are you familiar with the test directions and the types of questions in the test?

❑ Are you familiar with the recommended test-taking strategies and tips?

❑ Have you worked through the practice test questions at a pace similar to that of an actual test?

❑ If you are repeating a Praxis Series™ Assessment, have you analyzed your previous score report to determine areas where additional study and test preparation could be useful?

The Day of the Test

You should end your review a day or two before the actual test date. The day of the test you should

- Be well rested

- Take photo identification with you

- Take blue or black ink pens (pencils are not appropriate for a constructed-response test)

- Take your admission ticket, letter of authorization, mailgram or telegram with you

- Eat before you take the test to keep your energy level up

- Wear layered clothing; room temperature may vary

- Be prepared to stand in line to check in or to wait while other test takers are being checked in

You can't control the testing situation, but you can control yourself. Stay calm. The supervisors are well trained and make every effort to provide uniform testing conditions, but don't let it bother you if the test doesn't start exactly on time. You will have the full amount of time once it does start.

Think of preparing for this test as training for an athletic event. Once you've trained, prepared, and rested, give it everything you've got. Good luck.

Appendix A
Study Plan Sheet

► ► ► ► ► ► ► ► ► ► ►

Study Plan Sheet

See chapter 1 for suggestions about using this Study Plan Sheet.

			STUDY PLAN			
Content covered on test	How well do I know the content?	What material do I have for studying this content?	What material do I need for studying this content?	Where could I find the materials I need?	Dates planned for study of content	Dates completed

Appendix B
For More Information

▶　▶　▶　▶　▶　▶　▶　▶　▶　▶　▶　▶

ETS offers additional information to assist you in preparing for the Praxis Series™ Assessments. *Tests at a Glance* materials and the *Registration Bulletin* are both available without charge (see below to order). You can also obtain more information from our Web site: www.ets.org/praxis.

General Inquires

Phone: 800-772-9476, 609-771-7395 (Monday-Friday, 8:00 A.M. to 7:45 P.M., Eastern time)

Fax: 609-771-7906

Extended Time

If you have a learning disability or if English is not your primary language, you can apply to be given more time to take your test. The *Registration Bulletin* tells you how you can qualify for extended time.

Disability Services

Phone: 866-387-8602, 609-771-7780

Fax: 609-771-7165

TTY (for deaf or hard-of-hearing callers): 609-771-7714

Mailing Address

ETS–The Praxis Series™
P.O. Box 6051
Princeton, NJ 08541-6051

Overnight Delivery Address

ETS–The Praxis Series™
Distribution Center
225 Phillips Blvd.
Ewing, NJ 08628-7435